ABOUT THE AU[T]

Donna Crous is a South African based in Jersey, Channel Islands. Shortly after arriving in the UK in 2014, she started her blog www.eighty20nutrition.com, which went on to become an award-winning site. After qualifying as a Primal Blueprint Health Coach and working with clients, she realised that her passions and strengths lie in recipe creation and photography. In 2017 Donna was the overall winner of UK Paleo Blogger of the Year, runner up for Best Recipe Award and was a finalist in the UK Allergy Blog Awards. She has also been a regular contributor to *Gluten-Free Heaven*, *Vegan Food* and *Living* and *Thrive* magazines.

In 2017 Donna won third place in the blogging category of The Pink Lady Food Photographer of the Year Awards, which catapulted her career in food photography. She now works closely with authors and publishers by cooking, styling and photographing their recipes for publications and books. She is a regular guest speaker for The Photography Show, held annually in Birmingham, and runs talks and workshops for Nikon School of Photography and camera clubs around the UK. Her work is regularly featured in international photography magazines and national newspapers.

In 2020 Donna was appointed as the first Nikon UK and Europe Ambassador for food photography; she is also a Rotolight Master of Light.

Donna is mum to Gemma and Kyra, and wife to Derek.

Her photography portfolio can be viewed on www.donnacrous.com

A Healthier Family for Life

STRESS-FREE FEASTS FOR A MULTI-DIET FAMILY

Donna Crous

ROBINSON

ROBINSON

First published in Great Britain in 2021 by Robinson

A CIP catalogue record for this book is available from the British Library.

ISBN 978-1-47214-411-9

Designed by Andrew Barron @Thextension

Typeset in Adelle and Adelle Sans

Printed and bound in Great Britain by Bell and Bain Ltd, Glasgow.

Papers used by Robinson are from well-managed forests and other responsible sources.

Robinson
An imprint of Little, Brown Book Group
Carmelite House, 50 Victoria Embankment, London EC4Y 0DZ

An Hachette UK Company
www.hachette.co.uk
www.littlebrown.co.uk

The recommendations given in this book are solely intended as education and should not be taken as medical advice.

Dedication

My love goes out to parents trying to change their family's eating habits for the benefit of our future generation, to the many parents today who are questioning and challenging the traditional healthy-eating guidelines, what our food contains and where it comes from. Keep going, and be the change.

 To my guys Derek, Gemma, Kyra (and fur babies Jack and Lola), thank you for being open to making the crazy food changes I proposed so many years back – I love you more than life itself!

Eggs and vegetables are medium sized unless otherwise stated.

Free-range eggs are recommended, organic if possible.

Choose organic ingredients if you can.

Nuts are raw unless otherwise stated.

Fruits and vegetables used unpeeled should be washed.

Vegans should choose the vegan alternatives given in the ingredients lists.

Those following a keto diet should choose the keto alternative in the ingredients lists.

CONTENTS

Vegetables, Salads & Side Dishes

Drinks

INTRODUCTION

When I qualified as a health coach, I wanted to change the world – well, healthwise at least. I started to work with clients, and I very quickly learned that even though we all know that diet (and, obviously, exercise) is so important for optimal health, many people have no clue how to cook, which is where it all starts: in the kitchen. If they can cook, however, they are often stuck in a rut of cooking the same simple meals day in and day out until they become bored and break out the junk food. I stopped working with clients because I realised that the way in which I wanted to change the world was by teaching and sharing how to cook healthy, tasty meals with variety. I'm passionate about creating healthier, wholefood alternatives to store-bought highly processed food, because I believe that everyone should be able to enjoy their favourite treat, whether they are five or 105.

I've always had a passion for food – not just the healthy type, but all types. As a child, my favourite book was my mum's cookery book that I would page through and study the images. Clearly, it was foreshadowing my career in recipe design and food photography.

I really do have my mum to thank for my career, but this is not the traditional story of us spending time together in the kitchen baking or sharing age-old family recipes. It's more that my mum hated cooking so much that at the age of 14 I stepped up and decided to rescue her (and the family) by taking over the task of cooking our meals. As she had no interest in cooking, she also had no interest in owning any cookery books, besides the one that I loved, which was a wedding gift. With no knowledge of cooking, I learned to create dishes for our family using the ingredients available to me. I wasn't aware of it at the time, but through my regular meal preparation I learned many basic, foundational cooking skills – and a few unconventional ones since I was self-taught. Many adults don't possess cooking skills, due to the convenience of takeout, ready-made meals or, understandably, because they might be busy parents who don't want to mess up the kitchen.

My beautiful mum, Carol, sadly passed away from cancer in 2010 at the age of 63, and watching her fight so bravely and then dealing with our loss made me realise that I had to make changes for my little family. My family needed an intervention. My daughter Kyra was battling with health and weight issues, Gemma was on medication for ADHD, and my husband Derek and I were starting to suffer with niggling aches and pains and, of course, the dreaded middle-age spread. We changed our ways and, I won't lie, it certainly wasn't always easy, but we have never looked back.

As my girls have grown older, I've found that I'm less in control of how they eat. They still follow healthy diets but in very different versions. Gemma is now vegan, Kyra follows a low-carb, keto diet, and Derek and myself are closer to a Paleo diet, or our own version of it. All of us are gluten-, dairy- and processed sugar-free. I know it might seem crazy that we are all following different diets, but the reality is that these days many families live like this, be it through varying diet choices or because of intolerances. The way we eat in our family really isn't something out of the ordinary at all, which is why I decided to write *A Healthier Family for Life*.

Halfway through writing this book my world was rocked when I was diagnosed with breast cancer. I was 46 and believed myself to be bulletproof. The fact that I was otherwise in perfect health made me question everything I knew about health and nutrition. I now know that even though I still got cancer, my years of healthy eating had built up a body and cell system strong enough to endure the treatments, medications and surgeries that would follow over the coming year. I can proudly say that a year later I was given the all-clear by my doctors at the Royal Surrey County Hospital, and my gratitude goes to them. A huge thank you is also due to my friend and functional health coach, Darryl Edwards, who worked closely with me on the nutrition and exercise side. As much as I trusted my doctors, I knew that a huge part of my recovery and future prevention was also up to me and my lifestyle.

This book is not only a collection of my family's favourite recipes, but it's also a nod to beautiful fresh produce and the farmers who grow it. It's a high-five to all the parents trying to create interesting and exciting yet healthy dishes for their family. It's an A* for everyone willing to challenge what they have been taught in the past about healthy eating and question where our food comes from, how it is raised and what goes into it.

This book is not a diet book, it's not a weight-loss book and it's definitely not trying to be judgemental or evangelical about any specific diet. I believe that if you are reading this, you are ready to make a change or you have made a change already, or perhaps you too hate cooking and have been given this as a gift. Whatever the reason, I wish you a happy and healthier family for life!

Donna Crous

Ingredients for Healthy Eating

"Getting outside in nature and eating real food are two of the best medicines available to us. Vital for mental, emotional and physical health and even better when shared with people you love. Remember to seek joy when taking your daily prescription!

Darryl Edwards, bestselling author of *Animal Moves* and publisher at primalplay.com

WHAT IS IT, AND WHERE DO I FIND IT?

My most frequently asked question about my recipes is 'What is it, and where do I find it?' Navigating the minefield of healthy eating and alternative ingredients is really tricky. I totally understand why people give a healthy meal plan a go then fail a few weeks later; it can often feel as if some recipes are written in a foreign language when it comes to ingredients that are not mainstream. Cassava flour, nutritional yeast flakes and coconut aminos are all common ingredients used throughout this book, but they are not everyday ingredients. You might be surprised to know, however, that many of these ingredients can be found in your supermarket, but for some you might have to venture to your local health shop or hit the online shops.

You might be wondering, however, why there is such an extensive list of 'different' ingredients, and you might even be tempted to stick to the standard ingredients that you already have in your cupboard. I'm a strong believer that anything we eat should contribute a nutritional benefit to our body and I have chosen all the ingredients with this in mind. Taking sugar as an example, pure cane sugar that you buy in the supermarket is a highly refined ingredient, and the more highly refined an ingredient is, the worse it is for your health. By switching to less- or zero-processed sweeteners, such as raw local honey, high-grade maple syrup, coconut sugar or fresh dates, you will be consuming valuable nutrients and vitamins as well as enjoying the sweetness – plus they will be delicious and add a beautiful flavour to your food.

Even though none of my family members are coeliac, over the years we have all struggled with different side effects from gluten, but once we stopped eating regular flour (including store-bought gluten-free products), we discovered that many of the issues that we experienced later disappeared. Alternative baking is as much a science as it is an art. The flours that I have used in these recipes are all wheat- and grain-free and have been selected for their higher fibre content, healthy fats or low-carb properties, therefore they are not only great tasting but also gut friendly and far less processed than regular flour. (Please note: these flours cannot be substituted, as they all function in different ways.) As much as it is an investment, it's worthwhile stocking your pantry with a bag of each of these flours.

Cassava flour

Made from ground dehydrated cassava root (also known as yuca, manioc and tapioca), cassava is a wholefood flour, which means that the whole root is used; it is washed, baked and milled, which allows it to retain its fibre, protein, vitamins and minerals. Do be aware, however, that it is carb-heavy, which will be relevant if you are following a low-carb diet. This is a great alternative flour to work with as it can be replaced 1:1 with regular flour and is incredibly versatile. I purchase mine from my health shop (I asked them to stock it) or online and the brand that I have used throughout this book is Tiana.

Almond flour

I talk about almond flour throughout this book; it's simply fine-milled or ground almonds. I purchase my almond flour from Costco in 1.36kg bags, but ground almonds, which you will find in the baking section of your supermarket, are totally adequate. Do be careful not to overwork almond flour or ground almonds; being a ground-up nut it will release oil and can easily turn into almond butter.

Coconut flour

Very high in fibre, coconut flour absorbs liquid efficiently and can only be used in recipes that have a high moisture content. It's a tricky flour to work with, because just one teaspoon can make a huge difference to a recipe. It's low-carb, so it is great to use in a keto diet. I get mine from the flour section of my local supermarket.

Tapioca starch

This starch comes from ground cassava (see above), but it has a different texture and functionality, so is not to be used as a substitute for cassava flour. It adds elasticity to baking or is used as a thickener for sauces. It is high in carbs. You can find it in health stores and online.

Arrowroot powder

A great alternative to cornflour, arrowroot is dehydrated and ground arrowroot tuber. Since it is mostly starch, it is also high in carbohydrates. You can find it in the baking section in your supermarket (near to the bicarbonate of soda or baking yeasts).

Nutritional yeast flakes

This is not the regular kind of yeast that we use for baking bread; it's deactivated yeast and a delicious, dairy-free alternative to cheese, because it has a nutty, cheesy, savoury flavour. Fortified varieties are a great source of vitamin B12 and therefore ideal for a vegan diet (which is lacking in this vital vitamin). Find it in the gluten-free or health section of your supermarket.

Coconut aminos

Made from the fermented sap of coconut palm and sea salt, coconut aminos is a soya-, wheat- and gluten-free alternative to soy sauce. Ideal for those with food intolerances, it is easy to find in your health store or online.

Coconut sugar

Made from the coconut palm tree, coconut sugar is light brown in colour and has a strong and delicious caramel taste. Coconut sugar undergoes little processing, so it retains some of its vitamins, minerals, fibre and antioxidants. Be cautious though, as it still has the same number of calories as regular sugar, so use it sparingly. (Note that if you are following

a low-carb or keto diet, you will need to limit the use of coconut sugar.)
It can often be found in the sugar section of your local supermarket or
health stores.

Medjool dates

Although high in natural sugar, Medjool dates provide a punch of fibre,
which research shows is good for maintaining a healthy gut microbiome.
Medjool dates are a fresh fruit (not the dried ones found in the baking
section) and can be found in the fresh produce section of your supermarket or greengrocer. Keep them in the fridge or freezer to stay fresh.
Note that I have used fresh dates throughout this book, but if you are
unable to get fresh dates, dried unsweetened dates, soaked in warm water
until soft, will work well.

Harissa paste/spice

A North African spicy red paste or powder, harissa is a tasty combination
of red chillies, peppers, garlic and vinegar, and it adds a more intense
flavour than regular chilli paste. Not all pastes are made the same, and
some can be extremely spicy. The paste can be found in the Middle
Eastern section of supermarkets and the powder will be in the spice racks.

Blackstrap molasses

This dark, viscous liquid is the by-product of the sugar-cane refining
process. Don't worry, though, it's the good stuff and has the lowest sugar
content of any sugar-cane product. Actually, it has numerous health
benefits, as it contains a range of vital vitamins and minerals. Find it
in health stores and online.

Raw cacao vs cocoa

Raw cacao is made from fermented, dried and unroasted cacao beans,
whereas cocoa is processed at a higher temperature and often contains
sugar and dairy products. Find raw cacao in the baking section (not the
hot drink section) of your supermarket or health store.

Cocoa butter

Also called cacao butter or theobroma oil, cocoa butter is the creamy
yellow-white fat extracted through cold-pressing cocoa beans. Cocoa
butter is fast turning into a keto or low-carb favourite due to its numerous

health benefits when used both internally and externally. You can find it in larger health stores or online. It lasts for up to three years when stored in a cool dry place.

Avocado oil

Avocado oil is also the safest oil recommended for cooking, as it has the highest smoke point of all oils, around 250°C. The smoke point is the temperature that an oil starts to smoke in the pan and the structure then changes, both changing the flavour and creating free radicals which are damaging to your health. It has a delicious butter flavour and is a great alternative for dairy-free cooking and baking. You can find it in the oil section of your supermarket.

Raw apple cider vinegar

Made from fermented apples and water, raw, unfiltered, apple cider vinegar contains a cloudy substance that floats around in it, called the 'mother', which is formed during fermentation and is completely safe to consume. Some larger supermarkets stock raw versions, but otherwise it can be found in health stores or online.

Coconut kefir milk

Coconut kefir milk is a probiotic and enzyme-rich dairy-free drink made by fermenting coconut milk and kefir granules. Similar to a drinking yogurt, it can differ in thickness depending on the brand. Larger super-markets are stocking different brands in the dairy-alternatives fridge section; otherwise there are recipes online, and kefir granules can be purchased from health stores so that you can make it yourself.

Kefir cheese

A healthier and tastier cream cheese, kefir cheese is a cultured soft cheese made from dairy milk and kefir cultures. I'm aware that this is a dairy-free book, but the good news for lactose-intolerant people is that kefir cultures consume lactose, converting it into lactic acid and making it easily digestible. Be aware though, this is not the case for those who have dairy allergies. Find it in the dairy cheese section or yogurt fridges of larger supermarkets and in health stores.

Pink salt

Pink Himalayan rock salt is more natural than regular table salt. Table salt is usually heavily refined and often mixed with anti-caking agents to prevent clumping. Pink salt does not usually contain artificial ingredients or additives and adds a more interesting flavour to food. It is naturally harvested and hand extracted from the Salt Range mountains in Pakistan and is believed to contain trace elements and minerals. It can be purchased in different degrees of coarseness; I prefer to use finely ground as it makes it easier for baking and measuring. Find it in health stores or online. Note: if you can't find pink salt, any form of sea salt or Celtic salt is perfect.

Herbal or seasoned salt

Typically a blend of sea salt and herbs, herbal or seasoned salt can be used as a finishing salt to impart an extra boost of flavour into the dish, without making it too salty. It's made of a combination of ground dried herbs and seasoning mixed with sea salt and just adds gorgeous flavour to any dish. Find an organic one in your local health store, online or in the health section of your supermarket. Herbamare is the brand I like to use, but there also many homemade recipes available online that are both delicious and cost effective.

Kombucha

This drink starts as a sweet, sugary tea, which is fermented using a 'scoby' (similar to the mother in raw apple cider vinegar, above) which transforms into a refreshing, fizzy drink. Don't worry about the sugar content, because the scoby bacteria and yeast eat most of the sugar, so it is relatively low in calories and sugar, making it a great alternative to fizzy carbonated beverages. My local supermarkets now stock a large kombucha section with a variety of different brands and flavours. Health stores stock them in the fridges.

Miso paste

This is the only soya product I use, because it is naturally fermented, which makes it easily digestible. Organic miso is also a great source of probiotics. Find it in the Asian section of your local supermarket or health store.

Extracts

Essential in any alternative baker's pantry is a selection of different naturally flavoured extracts. I have a collection of rose water, orange, peppermint, almond, coffee and, of course, vanilla. Be sure to buy a good-quality brand that is naturally extracted and free from chemical flavourings. Extracts are a worthwhile investment, because they last for ages and are great to have on hand for a fast flavour boost. Find them in the baking section of your supermarket.

Psyllium husk

Psyllium husk is made from the shells of the *Plantago ovata* seeds and is popular with gluten-free bakers because it's a great way to bind baked goods and makes it possible to handle the dough when rolling or shaping it. Make sure to get the husk and not the powder. Find it in larger health stores or online.

Agar-agar

The gelling agent agar-agar is made from seaweed and is used as a substitute for gelatin in a vegetarian or vegan diet. Although it is used as a gelatin substitute, there is a difference: agar-agar is more powerful than gelatin and has a firmer texture when set. One teaspoon of agar-agar powder is equivalent to eight teaspoons of gelatin powder. Find it in the baking section of your local supermarket or health store.

Grass-fed gelatin

Although regular gelatin can be used, gelatin from grass-fed animals is a superior product in quality and nutrition. As with selecting meat products, your gelatin should come from grass-fed, sustainably reared animals. Good-quality gelatin is made from collagen, which is a protein and essential for our connective tissues, healthy skin, gut function and healthy joints. Colourless and tasteless, it's a useful ingredient for binding ingredients in gluten-free baking. Although it might initially appear to be very expensive, the powder is fine and light, so one tin or packet will last for ages. This is a specialised product and only available online or in well-stocked health stores. I use a local gelatin from Ossa.

Breakfasts

My mum used to call these drop scones, but some people know them as Scotch pancakes; in South Africa they are called flapjacks, and I like to call them silver dollar pancakes after a family trip to the USA. They are delicious served as soon as they have been made, with a drizzle of Chocolate Sauce (page 172), Salted Caramel Sauce (page 171), whipped coconut cream, homemade Strawberry Jam (page 168) or Lemon Curd (page 167). They can also be served savoury – blini style – with scrambled egg and salmon or crispy bacon.

SILVER DOLLAR PANCAKES

DAIRY-FREE/GLUTEN-FREE/KETO/PALEO

MAKES 10

3 free-range eggs

3 tbsp coconut flour, sifted

1 tbsp arrowroot powder

1 tsp ground cinnamon

1 tsp vanilla extract

½ tsp gluten-free baking powder

avocado oil, for frying

TRY SOMETHING DIFFERENT

For a savoury option, substitute the cinnamon and vanilla extract with ½ tsp herbal salt.

1 Put all the ingredients, except the oil, in a mixing bowl and whisk together until well combined and lump-free. Allow this batter to stand for 10 minutes.

2 Heat 1 tsp oil in a non-stick frying pan over a medium heat. Drop in 1-tbsp dollops of the batter and flatten them slightly with the back of the spoon. Be careful not to crowd the pan, as it makes flipping them difficult.

3 Cook each pancake for 2 minutes on each side. Repeat until all the batter is finished. Serve.

This is a recipe that just keeps on giving. Crispy on the outside and soft and chewy inside, these crêpes can be used for so many different dishes: from a simple breakfast crêpe to lasagna sheets, wraps or even as a naan bread substitute to serve with a delicious curry. (It's absolutely essential that you use a good non-stick frying pan for best results.)

VEGAN CRÊPES

DAIRY-FREE/GLUTEN-FREE/PALEO/VEGAN

MAKES 6–8

250ml canned full-fat coconut milk

50g almond flour or ground almonds

75g tapioca flour

½ tsp pink salt for savoury or 1 tsp vanilla extract for sweet

TIP

Due to the nature of tapioca flour, this batter will be very sticky if it is not cooked properly. Ensure that the crêpe is golden brown and crispy on both sides, otherwise your crêpe stack will turn into a sticky ball.

1 Put all the ingredients in a mixing bowl and whisk well together. Heat a small non-stick frying pan over a high heat.

2 Pour the batter into the pan and swirl it around, covering the entire base. Cook until the edges start to curl up and you can easily jiggle a palette knife or an egg flipper underneath it, then flip the crêpe.

3 Cook on the other side until golden brown and crispy, then transfer to a plate or cooling rack. Repeat until all the batter is finished.

It is amazing what you can create using just one egg. I love using eggs in my photography as they are just so beautiful and they capture the light perfectly. As well as looking delicious in photographs, they are also extremely nutritious and an all-round achiever. This recipe is versatile and can be enjoyed as either savoury or sweet.

EGG PANCAKES

DAIRY-FREE/GLUTEN-FREE/KETO/PALEO

MAKES 6

6 large free-range eggs

1 tbsp avocado oil

berries, coconut yogurt and nuts, or cheese, ham and chopped tomatoes, to serve

FOR A SAVOURY PANCAKE

½ tsp herbal salt (Herbamare)

½ tsp Italian or mixed herbs

FOR A SWEET PANCAKE

1 tsp vanilla extract

1 tsp honey, or maple syrup or sweetener (optional, see Tip)

TIP

For a low-carb sweet option you can simply add the vanilla extract and omit the honey. Savoury pancakes are perfect as a lunchtime wrap filled with salad, chicken and mayo.

1 Put the eggs in a large bowl and whisk them together, then add either the sweet or savoury flavourings.

2 Wipe a non-stick frying pan with a piece of kitchen paper that has been dunked in avocado oil – you don't want the pan covered in oil, just a wiping. Heat the pan over a medium-high heat.

3 Pour enough egg mixture into the pan to cover the base, and swirl it around. Cook until the edges start to curl up, then flip it and cook for a few seconds on the other side. Transfer to a warm plate.

4 Continue until the egg mixture is finished. Serve with berries, coconut yogurt and nuts for a sweet option; or cheese, ham and chopped tomatoes for a savoury version.

As much as we all love a big bowl of Brussels sprouts with our Christmas lunch, we somehow always have a ton of leftovers. Let's be honest: nobody likes warmed-up sprouts the next day. It is one of those vegetables that is the last in the leftover bowl and invariably ends up being chucked away. Not anymore! With this recipe, you can reinvent your leftovers to create these delicious Turkish eggs, although you will definitely have to elbow a few supermarket shoppers out of the way for an extra bag of sprouts during your Christmas Eve shop.

TURKISH EGGS WITH BRUSSELS SPROUTS

DAIRY-FREE/GLUTEN-FREE/KETO/PALEO

SERVES 4

4 tbsp coconut oil or avocado oil

400g chopped, cooked Brussels sprouts, or fresh, sliced into chunks

2 small garlic cloves, crushed, or 1 tsp garlic granules

a pinch of pink salt

4 free-range eggs

½ tsp paprika

3 tbsp chilli oil

160ml coconut yogurt

nigella seeds, for sprinkling

toasted Keto Bread (page 192), to serve

TIP

You can also follow steps 1–2 of the recipe for The Best Brussels Sprouts – Ever! on page 132.

1 Heat 2 tbsp of the oil in a frying pan over a medium-high heat and cook the Brussels sprouts for 5–10 minutes until caramelised and soft (the cooking time will vary depending on whether they are being reheated or cooked from raw, so it's really a personal preference).

2 Add the garlic and salt, and cook for 2 minutes. Transfer to a plate or bowl and keep warm.

3 Heat the remaining 2 tbsp oil in the pan and fry the eggs to your liking, although ideally the yolks should be runny.

4 Mix together the paprika and chilli oil in a small bowl. Warm through the yogurt in a small saucepan over a medium heat or in a microwave on a medium heat for 1½ minutes.

5 Top the sprouts with the warmed yogurt, followed by the soft fried eggs and a drizzle of the paprika oil, then sprinkle with nigella seeds and serve with a slice of toasted Keto Bread.

If you haven't tasted duck eggs before, you are in for a treat! They are a level up from hen's eggs, as they are higher in omega-3 fats and are more nutrient dense. Besides their obvious larger size, they are just so incredibly delicious and creamy, and are perfect for boiled eggs and broccoli soldiers. It's important to note that all eggs (chicken, duck or quail) should come from well-raised fowl. I like to purchase all my eggs from local farmers' markets, farm stores or tables with honesty boxes.

DUCK EGGS WITH TENDERSTEM BROCCOLI SOLDIERS

DAIRY-FREE/GLUTEN-FREE/KETO/PALEO

SERVES 4

125g Tenderstem broccoli

4 free-range duck eggs

1 Fill a saucepan halfway with boiling water and return to the boil. Add the broccoli and cook for 2–3 minutes – you want it to be softened on the outside yet still have a crisp snap on the inside.

2 Using a slotted spoon, remove the broccoli and set aside.

3 Add the eggs to the boiling broccoli water and set the timer for 6 minutes for soft eggs or 9–12 minutes for hard eggs.

4 Serve with the broccoli for dunking into soft eggs or remove the hard-boiled eggs, immediately put them into a bowl of cold water then peel, cut in half and serve with the broccoli.

This is a mouthful both to say and to eat! Chakalaka (pronounced chuck-a-luck-ah), also known as Soweto chilli, originated in the townships of Johannesburg and its surrounding gold mines. Mineworkers coming off their shifts would cook tinned beans with tomatoes, vegetables and chilli to produce a warm and satisfying stew eaten with meat and mielie-meal (a coarse maize flour called pap). Today there are many variations of the recipe depending on the area and culture. Some use the chilli sauce peri-peri whereas others use a mild curry to add to the base flavour – the choice is entirely yours.

CHAKALAKA SHAKSHUKA EGGS

DAIRY-FREE/GLUTEN-FREE/KETO/PALEO

SERVES 4

2 tbsp avocado oil

1 onion, sliced

70g sliced cabbage (mix green and red if possible)

1 garlic clove, crushed

200g cherry tomatoes

1 red pepper, seeded and cut into 1cm strips

2 carrots, spiralised, or cut into ribbons or thinly sliced

4 free-range eggs

chopped fresh coriander or parsley, to garnish

FOR THE SAUCE

400ml passata

1 tsp paprika

1–2 tsp curry powder, or chilli powder or peri-peri sauce, to taste

1 tsp garlic granules

½ tsp ground ginger

½ tsp cayenne pepper

1 tbsp coconut sugar, or raw honey or sweetener

1 tsp pink salt

1 Preheat the oven to 180°C (160°C fan oven) Gas 4. Heat the oil in an ovenproof skillet or frying pan over a medium heat and fry the onion until soft.

2 Add the cabbage, garlic, tomatoes, red pepper and carrots, and cook until soft.

3 Mix the sauce ingredients together in a small bowl. then pour it over the veggie mix.

4 Bake the veggies and sauce for 25 minutes. Remove from the oven and make four dents in the chakalaka (or more if needed) and break the eggs into the dents.

5 Bake for 10 minutes for a deliciously soft, runny egg yolk. Sprinkle with chopped coriander or parsley before serving.

TIP

The eggs might still be slightly translucent when removed from the oven, but they will continue to cook. For a hard yolk, bake for 5 minutes more or until your preferred doneness.

My family dislike the name, but it really is the perfect title for this frittata. You know those times when you look into the fridge and see a whole load of veggies that are close to heading to the compost heap but you don't have the heart to chuck them just yet? Enter Clear-the-Fridge Frittata! Any veggies or leftover meals can be thrown into it, whether peppers, potatoes, leftover stew or roast chicken – they will get a revamp in this delicious dish. I've added a few ingredients that I regularly use in my frittatas, but feel free to change them and add anything from your fridge. It's ideal for breakfast, or served with a big garden salad for lunch or for casual dinners, or simply cut up and popped into lunchboxes.

CLEAR-THE-FRIDGE FRITTATA

DAIRY-FREE/GLUTEN-FREE/KETO/PALEO

SERVES 8–12

3 tbsp avocado oil, or olive oil or coconut oil, or as needed

250g bacon, chopped

1 red onion, sliced

1 red pepper, seeded and sliced (or other leftover veg)

1 orange pepper, seeded and sliced (or other leftover veg)

12 free-range eggs

3 tbsp vegan Parmesan cheese (see Friday Night Pizza, page 101) or nutritional yeast flakes

½ tsp pink salt

½ tsp Italian herbs

½ tsp chilli powder (optional)

1 Preheat the oven to 200°C (180°C fan oven) Gas 6 and grease an ovenproof dish. Heat 1 tbsp of the oil in a large frying pan over a medium heat and fry the bacon until crisp. Transfer to a plate and set aside, keeping the fat in the pan.

2 Add more oil if needed to the pan and fry the onion and peppers (or whatever leftover veg you find in the fridge) until soft. Return the bacon to the pan and mix with the vegetables.

3 Put the eggs in a bowl with 125ml water, the Parmesan, salt and the herbs and chilli, if using. Whisk together, then pour into the prepared dish.

4 Add the veggie and bacon mix, dotting it evenly around. Bake for 35–40 minutes until firm in the middle. Leave to cool before serving.

The is one of my favourite recipes to make up when we go to Sanbona game reserve, which is about three hours' drive out of Cape Town. Sanbona is a special place to our family and such a beautiful opportunity to get out into wide open spaces and up close with wild animals in their natural habitat. The combination of early mornings and fresh air makes everyone so hungry when out with their binoculars and cameras spotting wild animals, so a hearty breakfast when we stop for a coffee break goes down very well.

I prefer to make these the night before and then pop them in the fridge ready to go for our very early start. When we stop for a welcomed break, they go down such a treat, and it's just like having a compact and convenient mini English breakfast. You don't need to be heading out on safari to make these up – they are ideal for road trips, camping or simply for a breakfast on the run.

BAKED EGGS WITH PROSCIUTTO

DAIRY-FREE/GLUTEN-FREE/KETO/PALEO

SERVES 6

oil, for greasing

6 slices prosciutto or Parma ham

6 tsp Pesto (page 156), tomato sauce or mayonnaise

6 free-range eggs

1 Preheat the oven to 200°C (180°C fan oven) Gas 6. Spray or grease a six-cup muffin pan with oil. Line each cup with prosciutto, ensuring that you cover the base and sides.

2 Pop into each cup 1 tsp pesto, then use the back of a teaspoon to gently spread it over the prosciutto. Break an egg into each cup. Bake for 10 minutes for a soft runny yolk or 15 minutes for hard. Remove from the oven and allow to cool for 10 minutes, then gently use a knife to remove them from the baking pan. Enjoy either hot or cold.

What a great way to start the day with a tummy full of good food! This is when, as a parent, you are able to provide your children with a good start to a school day. By filling your children up with healthy fats as found in eggs, coconut and avocado oil this breakfast will keep them satiated for longer, helping them to concentrate better during classes.

CREAMY SCRAMBLED EGGS

DAIRY-FREE/GLUTEN-FREE/KETO/PALEO

SERVES 4

1 tbsp avocado oil

6 free-range eggs

125ml coconut cream, or coconut kefir, full-fat coconut milk or nut milk

1 tsp dried tarragon or mixed herbs

pink salt and ground black pepper

Keto Bread (page 192), to serve

1 Heat the oil in a frying pan over a medium heat. Whisk together the remaining ingredients in a bowl and season with salt and pepper to taste.

2 Pour the egg mixture into the pan. Using a spatula, constantly stir the mixture, scraping the sides and base.

3 Remove the eggs when cooked to your personal preference (we split ours in half, because some family members prefer theirs softer than others). Serve with a slice of bread.

This is my tasty, grain-free and more nutritious version of a much-loved classic English dish. Although this recipe does have a small amount of carbs, if your daily macros won't allow for it (if you are on a keto or low-carb diet), feel free to leave out the cassava flour and arrowroot powder.

I have chosen to add this to the breakfast line-up, but it's also great for a Sunday night dinner served with vegetables and caramelised or fried onions.

BREAKFAST TOAD-IN-THE-HOLE

DAIRY-FREE/GLUTEN-FREE/KETO/PALEO

SERVES 4-6

1 tsp plus 1 tbsp avocado oil

6 gluten-free pork sausages or 12 chipolatas

6 free-range eggs

100ml nut milk

1 tbsp arrowroot powder

2 tbsp cassava flour

1 tsp mustard powder

1 tsp gluten-free baking powder

½ tsp herbal salt (Herbamare) or pink salt

½ tsp dried oregano

a sprinkle of dried chilli flakes (optional)

a few fresh thyme sprigs, to serve

1 Preheat the grill in your oven – or preheat your grill, and your oven to 180°C (160°C fan oven) Gas 4. Coat the sausages in the 1 tsp oil and put them in an ovenproof dish.

2 Grill the sausages for 10 minutes or until starting to brown, turning half-way through cooking (they don't need to be cooked all the way through, this process is mainly to brown them).

3 Put the eggs in a bowl and add the milk, the 1 tbsp oil, the arrowroot powder, cassava flour, mustard powder, baking powder, salt, oregano and chilli flakes. Whisk together well.

4 Remove the sausages from the grill and change the oven setting to 180°C (160°C fan oven) Gas 4. Pour the egg mixture into the dish with the grilled sausages and, once the oven is ready, cook for 30 minutes.

5 When the timer is up, turn the oven back to grill and grill until crispy and golden.

6 Turn the grill off and open the door slightly for 5–10 minutes until ready to serve.

7 Serve with thyme sprigs.

Mackerel is a nutrient powerhouse loaded with healthy fats. If you want to pack a huge punch in a small package, make up these muffins and serve them for breakfast, lunch or dinner. They are easy to make; I simply purchase deboned, hot-smoked fillets from the deli section (where you find smoked salmon and other cold-cured fish) in my local supermarket. If you don't have any luck finding them, tinned mackerel fillets will also work well.

MACKEREL EGG MUFFINS

DAIRY-FREE/GLUTEN-FREE/KETO/PALEO

MAKES 6–8

200g filleted, hot-smoked mackerel fillets (or tinned fillets)

6 free-range eggs

125ml nut milk

½ tsp pink salt

a few dill sprigs, chopped

TIP

Serve with a dollop of Oyster Mayonnaise (page 163), if you like – it's utterly heavenly!

1 Preheat the oven to 180°C (160°C fan oven) Gas 4. Put 6–8 muffin cases into a muffin pan (depending on whether you want small muffins or larger ones).

2 Remove the skins from the smoked mackerel and mash the flesh with a fork.

3 Put the eggs, milk and salt in a bowl and whisk together.

4 Pour the egg mixture into the muffin cases and evenly distribute the mackerel between each case. Top with a sprinkle of dill, and bake for 30 minutes.

5 When the 30 minutes is up, switch off the oven and leave the door of the oven open with the muffins still inside for 5–10 minutes or until ready to serve (this just stops them from shrinking when they come out of the oven).

As much as I'm not a lover of boxed cereals, I understand the convenience factor, especially if you have little children. Mornings can be a whirlwind, and not everyone has the time or capacity to cook up a meal. Making this cereal in advance and storing it in a jar is perfect for busy mornings.

Mix up a portion with hot or cold milk to the desired consistency; some prefer it really runny, whereas others prefer it so thick that their spoon can stand up in it.

INSTANT CHOCOLATE CEREAL

DAIRY-FREE/GLUTEN-FREE/KETO/PALEO/VEGAN

MAKES A 750ML JAR

150g milled flaxseed

150g almond flour

50g coconut flour

50g raw cacao powder

100g pecan nuts or walnuts

50g hazelnuts

2 tsp ground cinnamon

4–6 tbsp coconut sugar or sweetener (optional)

TO SERVE

nut milk

honey, or maple syrup, sweetener, grated dark or raw chocolate, raisins or fresh berries (optional)

TIP

You can substitute the flaxseed by doubling the almond and coconut flour quantities.

1 Put all the ingredients into a food processor and whiz to make a crumb consistency.

2 Serve a portion mixed with nut milk until the desired consistency. You might want to add a drizzle of honey or even add raisins or fresh berries or a sprinkle of grated dark or raw chocolate. Store in a 750ml sealable jar in the pantry.

I've made this granola in many different shapes and forms over the years. Not only is it way cheaper than store-bought granola but it is also very rich and contains loads of good fats, so a smaller serving is needed for satiety. Do be cautious of how much you dish up because it is surprisingly filling.

DARK CHOCOLATE AND CRANBERRY GRANOLA

DAIRY-FREE/GLUTEN-FREE/KETO/PALEO/VEGAN

MAKES 700G

400g mixed nuts (choose your favourite or buy a mixed bag from the supermarket)

50g desiccated coconut

50g dried cranberries

50g shelled hemp seeds

3 tbsp coconut oil

2 tbsp raw honey, or maple syrup or powdered sweetener

2 tsp vanilla extract

2 tsp ground cinnamon

½ tsp ground ginger

40g dairy-free dark chocolate chips

TIP

The baking time might vary, and a close eye needs to be kept on it towards the end of the baking, because nuts can turn very quickly from done to burnt.

1 Preheat the oven to 180°C (160°C fan oven) Gas 4 and line a baking tray with baking paper or a silicon mat. In a food processor pulse the mixed nuts in a few short bursts (or chop them into smaller pieces – a variety of sizes is fine).

2 Tip into a large bowl, then add the coconut, cranberries and hemp seeds, and stir through.

3 Put the coconut oil, honey and vanilla extract in a small saucepan and melt together over a medium heat (or use a microwave), then stir in the cinnamon and ginger.

4 Pour the oil mixture over the nut mixture and stir well to coat the nuts completely.

5 Transfer the mixture to the prepared baking tray and bake for 20 minutes (see Tip). Remove from the oven and stir in the chocolate. Leave to cool completely, then store in a sealable glass jar.

When Gemma was in her teens, she studied at a college in London. London is about a 45-minute train ride into Waterloo from where we live, but the thing about Gemma is that she is a late riser and extremely slow in the mornings, both of which do not make for a fun morning trying to get a sleepy teenager to the train on time. In between all this chaos, breakfast would be missed and she would leave for a long day on an empty stomach. Even if I packed her a bowl of fruit or a cup of porridge, she would be too shy to eat it on a jam-packed train full of London-bound commuters. For this reason I developed this recipe: a simple bar that could be popped into her coat pocket and munched on throughout the morning.

CRUNCHY ON-THE-GO GRANOLA BARS

DAIRY-FREE/GLUTEN-FREE/PALEO/VEGAN

MAKES 8

10 fresh Medjool dates, or dried unsweetened dates soaked in warm water until soft, pitted and chopped

200g mixed nuts

50g sunflower seeds

50g pumpkin seeds

50g desiccated or flaked coconut

1 egg or 2 tsp psyllium husk mixed with 60ml water

1 tbsp vanilla extract

4 tbsp coconut oil, melted

½ tsp pink salt

FOR THE CHOCOLATE TOPPING (OPTIONAL)

70g dairy-free dark chocolate chips

1 tsp coconut oil

a sprinkle of pink salt flakes

1 Preheat the oven to 170°C (150°C fan oven) Gas 3 and grease or line with baking paper a 23 x 23cm baking tin or ovenproof dish. Add the ingredients to a food processor and pulse in a few short bursts until the ingredients are well mixed yet still chunky. You don't want it turning into a gooey paste!.

2 Transfer to the prepared baking tin and press down firmly with the base of a ramekin until it's flat and even. Bake for 25 minutes. Remove from the oven and leave to cool.

3 To make the topping, melt the chocolate chips and coconut oil together in a heatproof bowl over a pan of gently simmering water (or use a microwave). Drizzle over the top of the baked mixture and sprinkle with salt crystals. Leave to cool, then cut into eight bars (or smaller if you prefer).

When I was at boarding school in Polokwane in the northern parts of South Africa, we used to have a similar dish that was served on Sunday nights called *melkkos* (milk food), which is a traditional Afrikaans porridge or dessert made with milk, flour and butter. This healthier version has become Kyra's favourite breakfast dish on a cold winter's morning. Loaded with fats, protein and carbohydrates, this porridge is just so delicious and comforting. Being a smooth porridge, it is perfect for tactile defensive eaters, who usually don't like the texture of regular porridge. You just can't go wrong with this in the tummy first thing in the morning (or even as a healthy pudding).

BELLY-WARMING MILK PORRIDGE

DAIRY-FREE/GLUTEN-FREE/PALEO

SERVES 2–4

400ml canned full-fat coconut milk

2 tbsp avocado oil or olive oil

3 egg yolks

3 tbsp tapioca flour

2 tbsp cassava flour

1–2 tbsp raw honey, or maple syrup or sweetener, to taste

2 tsp vanilla extract

1 tsp almond extract

a sprinkle of cinnamon, for topping

TIP

If you do end up with lumps and bumps, push the mixture through a sieve to remove them. This happens when the hob is a tad too hot.

1 Put 300ml of the milk in a saucepan over a medium heat and add the oil. Gently heat together.

2 Meanwhile, combine the remaining ingredients, and the remaining milk, and whisk together well.

3 Once the milk has warmed and is starting to steam, add the other ingredients and immediately turn the heat down to medium-low.

4 Using a small hand whisk, stir continuously until the mixture starts to thicken. Please don't be tempted to turn up the temperature, or you will end up with scrambled eggs.

5 The mixture will change from slightly frothy to very shiny before starting to thicken.

6 Once thick, remove from the heat and serve warm with a sprinkle of cinnamon.

A Healthier Family for Life | Breakfasts

As a child I never turned down a bowl of hot, creamy oat porridge. I have such happy memories of chatting with my grandma over a bowl of oats with cream and tons of sugar. I know that oat porridge is definitely a dish missed by those who follow a grain-free and low-carb diet, but as with most well-loved and traditional dishes, a healthier or alternative version can always be found.

'OAT' PORRIDGE

DAIRY-FREE/GLUTEN-FREE/KETO/PALEO/VEGAN

SERVES 1–2

30g mixed nuts or nut of your choice

25g flaked almonds

35g pumpkin seeds

2 tbsp sesame seeds

25g dried coconut

1 tsp coconut flour

250ml nut milk, or full-fat coconut milk or Pumpkin Seed Mylk (page 265)

1 tsp vanilla extract

coconut cream, raw honey (for non-vegans), berries and ground cinnamon, to serve

TIP

Make up a large batch of the dry ingredients and store them in a glass jar in your fridge for up to two weeks. This will make mornings much quicker having it pre-mixed and readily available.

1 Put the nuts in a food processor or blender and add the seeds, dried coconut and coconut flour, then pulse in short bursts a few times (don't overdo it – you don't want flour or, worse, a paste).

2 Pour the milk into a saucepan and add the vanilla, then heat slowly over a medium-low heat. Once it's steaming, add the nut mixture, and bring to a gentle boil. Serve with coconut cream, raw honey, berries and cinnamon.

This is the last recipe in my breakfast section, and I'm going to let you in on a little secret: I've never been a big breakfast eater. As a food photographer, I'm surrounded by food all day long. I'm either up early frying onions and garlic for a cookery book or working on my own recipes. I have the luxury of snacking all day if I want to, so instead of eating a full breakfast I'll make up a glass of green juice to get my day started.

Smoothies, especially ready-made ones, are not something I would recommend, as they are usually packed with delicious, yet high-sugar, fruit. I feel the same way about juicing: not only can it be full of very high-sugar fruits, but the most important part – the fibre – is usually disposed of. It's important to include the fibre and use the whole fruit or vegetables, where possible with the peel included, as it helps with breaking down the sugars and aids digestion.

GREEN JUICE

DAIRY-FREE/GLUTEN-FREE/KETO/PALEO/VEGAN

SERVES 2

1 large handful of baby spinach

5 sprigs of mint, or more to taste, chopped (include the stalks, but remove any woody, hard bits on the end)

½ green apple, cored and unpeeled

½–1 lime, to taste, peeled, chopped into pieces

a chunk of fresh ginger, to taste, peeled

10cm wedge of cucumber, chopped into chunks

250ml coconut water

1 Blitz all the ingredients together in a blender or food processor and enjoy this electric-green shock of goodness!

TIP

Play around with different quantities of ingredients – it totally depends on your personal taste preference.

Main Meals

Although bobotie is a traditional South African sweet curry dish, we seldom ate it when we lived in South Africa. Since moving to the UK, however, I make it on a regular basis. Traditionally, it is made by soaking bread in milk, then mixing it through the meat mixture, but my version is grain-free and, trust me, even a true South African wouldn't notice the absence of soggy bread.

BOBOTIE WITH YELLOW CAULI-RICE

DAIRY-FREE/GLUTEN-FREE/KETO/PALEO

SERVES 6–8

1 tbsp avocado oil

1 small onion, chopped

1kg minced beef

1½ tsp garlic granules or powder

2 tsp curry powder

2 tbsp garam masala

1 tsp ground mixed spice

½ tsp ground cumin

1½ tsp ground turmeric

1 tsp chilli powder

1 tsp mixed herbs

1½ tsp pink salt

2 tbsp raw honey, or coconut sugar or sweetener

30g raisins or sultanas

4 tbsp raw apple cider vinegar

FOR THE EGG TOPPING

3 free-range eggs

250ml nut milk

125ml coconut cream

3 bay leaves

FOR THE YELLOW CAULI-RICE

500g cauliflower, chopped into chunks

140g cashew nuts

3 tsp ground turmeric

½ tsp pink salt

1 tsp garlic granules

1 tsp ground cinnamon

½ tsp ground cumin

3 tbsp avocado oil

1 Preheat the oven to 180°C (160°C fan oven) Gas 4. Heat the oil in a large frying pan over a medium-high heat and cook the onion for 5 minutes or until soft. Add the mince and cook quickly to brown it.

2 Add the garlic, spices, herbs, salt and honey, and stir into the meat. Cook for a further 5 minutes to allow the spices to activate (it should smell heavenly by now).

3 Add the raisins, vinegar and 100ml water, and mix through.

4 Remove from the heat and transfer the mince to an ovenproof baking dish.

5 Using the back of a wooden spoon, flatten the mince into the dish, making sure to push it down hard and firm.

6 To make the topping, crack the eggs into a bowl and add the milk and cream. Whisk together, then pour evenly over the top of the meat. Arrange the bay leaves on top and bake for 45 minutes.

7 To make the yellow cauli-rice, put the cauliflower into a food processor and add the cashew nuts, turmeric, salt, garlic granules, cinnamon and cumin. Blitz together until you have rice-sized granules.

8 Heat the oil in a frying pan over a medium-high heat, and cook the cauli-rice, stirring regularly, for 5 minutes or until softened but with a bite. Serve with the bobotie.

My guys love this dish. They don't usually get excited about loads of veggies, but because they are hidden in this dish it's my safeguard when I have no idea what to make for dinner. It is utterly delicious with rose veal, but lamb mince or any other type of meat will work beautifully as well. Make sure your cauliflower sauce is super-smooth – that's the trick to hiding your vegetables and making the family believe it is just a creamy sauce!

MOUSSAKA WITH CAULIFLOWER BÉCHAMEL SAUCE

DAIRY-FREE/GLUTEN-FREE/KETO/PALEO

SERVES 4–6

2 firm aubergines

avocado oil or coconut oil, for frying

1 onion, chopped

1–2 garlic cloves, to taste, crushed

500g minced rose veal, or lamb or beef

pink salt

250ml tomato passata

1–2 tbsp harissa paste

800g cauliflower, cut into florets

200ml tinned coconut cream

1 tbsp herbal salt (Herbamare), to taste

45g nutritional yeast flakes

green salad, to serve

1 Slice the larger aubergine into discs 1cm thick. Slice the smaller aubergine into discs 2mm thick (really thin).

2 Soak the aubergines in two separate bowls of lightly salted water for 10 minutes.

3 Remove and pat dry with kitchen paper.

4 Heat a little oil for shallow frying in a large frying pan over a high heat. Fry the thicker slices of aubergine on both sides, adding more oil if needed, then transfer to a plate.

5 Add more oil and fry the thinner aubergine slices. When ready, keep them separate from the large ones (bear with me, this will make sense when assembling).

6 Add a little more oil and fry the onion for 5 minutes or until softened, then add the garlic, stir well, then add the meat.

7 Lightly brown the meat, and add ½ tsp pink salt, the passata and harissa paste, mixing well.

8 Cook over a high heat for 10 minutes, then reduce the heat to medium-low and simmer gently while you get on with prepping the sauce. Meanwhile, preheat the oven to 180°C (160°C fan oven) Gas 4.

(continued over page)

9 To make the cauliflower béchamel sauce, fill a saucepan halfway with boiling water, and add a pinch of salt and the cauliflower florets. Boil until very soft. Strain well, and (either using an immersion stick blender or transferring into a blender or smoothie maker) blend with the coconut cream, herbal salt and half the nutritional yeast flakes until very smooth.

10 Lay the thick slices of aubergine over the base of an ovenproof dish, then add the meat and top with the cauliflower sauce. (One layer of each is perfect.) Sprinkle the remaining nutritional yeast flakes over the cauliflower sauce. Top with the thin aubergine slices and bake for 30 minutes. Serve with a big green salad.

My grandfather, Mannie, was born in Madeira and moved to South Africa when he was a young adult. He gave up most of his Portuguese heritage in an attempt to conform, even changing the spelling of his surname. Because of this he, sadly, did not even teach his children to speak Portuguese. Thankfully, the one thing he was able to teach and share with us is this age-old family recipe for pork. In Madeira it is known as *Carne' Vinha d'alhos*, or garlic and wine-marinated pork, and it is traditionally made with a pork loin and served on Christmas Day. This is a regular dish in our house – we love it on Christmas Day and any other day of the year.

When buying pork, remember always to buy free-range or organic whenever possible. It is important that the animal has had a chance to move around freely and forage, such as eating acorns, instead of being locked up and confined to a small area. Not only does this freedom improve the quality of the meat but also its taste.

Ideally, this dish should be started a day before serving and left to marinate overnight in the fridge. If you don't have the luxury of time, marinating a few hours before serving is best.

MADEIRAN PORK BELLY

DAIRY-FREE/GLUTEN-FREE/KETO/PALEO

SERVES 4–6

250ml raw apple cider vinegar

5–6 garlic cloves, to taste, crushed

1 tbsp dried chilli flakes, or to taste

1.5kg higher-welfare pork belly

2–3 tbsp table salt

avocado oil, for roasting

1 tsp pink salt

1 The day before, mix the vinegar, garlic and chilli flakes in a baking dish large enough to hold the pork belly.

2 Score the top of the pork belly (the thick skin), then sprinkle with table salt to cover the skin (this is to draw moisture out of the skin so that it becomes crispy when cooked).

3 Carefully transfer the pork belly to the dish putting it meat-side down in the vinegar. Make sure the vinegar does not cover the skin, just the meat; if the level is too high, remove some of the vinegar.

4 Cover and leave overnight in the fridge (it can be made up to 1 hour before, but the more time the better). Remove from the fridge 1 hour before cooking to allow the pork to return to room temperature.

(continued over page)

5 Preheat the oven to 200°C (180°C fan oven) Gas 6. Pick up the pork (it's going to get messy with the marinade, but bear with me) then run just the skin section under a tap to wash off the salt crust. Pat the skin dry with kitchen paper and put the pork back into the vinegar marinade, meat-side down.

6 Rub the skin with a touch of oil and sprinkle with the pink salt. Roast for 1 hour.

7 Increase the oven temperature to 230°C (210°C fan oven) Gas 8 and continue roasting for 10 minutes.

8 Change to a low grill setting and cook until the crackling starts to blister and bubble.

9 Remove from the oven and discard the vinegar. Cut the pork into chunks and serve.

Cottage pie or shepherd's pie: what is the difference? It's quite simply the type of minced meat used: cottage is made with beef and shepherd's with lamb. This recipe breaks all the traditions and uses turkey and bacon. Having strayed from tradition by topping it with a cauli mash instead of traditional mashed potatoes, I decided to take it one step further and add a crumb topping, which isn't even a thing on a traditional cottage or shepherd's pie, but it should be, because it adds a great, crispy, crunchy element to the dish.

Don't feel you have to use turkey mince – feel free to experiment with different types of minced meat that you have available.

TURKEY AND BACON COTTAGE PIE

DAIRY-FREE/GLUTEN-FREE/KETO/PALEO

SERVES 4–6

300g smoked back bacon (hold two rashers back for the topping)

1 tbsp avocado oil

½ onion, chopped

2 garlic cloves, crushed

500g minced turkey

½ tsp pink salt

1 tsp Italian herbs, or to taste

½ tsp paprika, or to taste

100ml tomato passata

60ml tomato purée

steamed vegetables or a green salad, to serve

FOR THE CAULI MASH

400g cauliflower, chopped

60ml coconut kefir or coconut cream

1 tsp English mustard

1 tsp herbal salt (Herbamare)

FOR THE TOPPING (OPTIONAL)

2 bacon rashers (from the total above)

50g almond flour

3 tbsp nutritional yeast flakes

1 Use either a food processor or a knife to finely chop the bacon rashers, except the two for the topping.

2 Heat the oil in a frying pan over a medium-high heat and fry the onion for 5 minutes or until soft, then add the garlic and bacon. Cook until the bacon is browned, then add the turkey mince and cook until browned.

3 Add the salt, herbs, paprika, passata and tomato purée. Return to the boil, then reduce the heat and simmer gently for 10 minutes. Have a taste, and add extra herbs or paprika if necessary. Meanwhile, preheat the oven to 180°C (160°C fan oven) Gas 4.

4 To make the cauli mash, steam or boil the cauliflower until soft, then drain well and mash with the kefir, mustard and salt. Set aside.

5 To make the topping, put the bacon, almond flour and nutritional yeast flakes in a food processor and blitz to make the crumb.

6 Transfer the filling to an ovenproof dish, then top with the cauli mash and then the topping. Bake for 30–45 minutes until the crumble is crispy and the mash is golden brown. Serve hot with steamed vegetables or a green salad.

This is a beautiful combination of cultures: Korean dangmyeon noodles (also known as glass noodles) are deliciously healthy, grain-free noodles made from sweet-potato starch and water, and carbonara is the epitome of Italian cuisine: a creamy smooth sauce served over pasta. Why not take the best from different cultures and combine them to create a delicious grain-free, plant-based dish? The noodles can be found in Asian supermarkets or online. If you can't find them, use folded rice noodles, which are easily available in the Asian section of your local supermarket.

SWEET POTATO GLASS NOODLES WITH CARBONARA

DAIRY-FREE/GLUTEN-FREE/PALEO/VEGAN

SERVES 6–8

2 cauliflowers, chopped into even-sized chunks

1 tbsp herbal salt (Herbamare), or to taste

30g nutritional yeast flakes, or to taste

160ml coconut cream

2 tbsp avocado oil

300g chestnut mushrooms

2–3 garlic cloves, to taste, crushed

100g frozen peas

400g sweet potato noodles (dangmyeon noodles) or folded rice noodles

TIP

Make this keto by substituting the noodles with spiralised courgettes. As this dish is low in protein, feel free to add grilled chicken, fried bacon or even cooked prawns; for vegans, blend silken or smooth tofu into the cauliflower purée.

1 Steam or boil the cauliflower until very soft, and drain well. Add the cauliflower to a blender or food processor and add the herbal salt, nutritional yeast flakes and coconut cream.

2 Blend until smooth and creamy, then taste and add any further seasoning if needed. Transfer to a saucepan, cover and keep warm over a medium-low setting, stirring regularly.

3 Heat the oil in a frying pan over a high heat and cook the chestnut mushrooms and garlic for 3–5 minutes or until soft and golden, then set aside.

4 Microwave the frozen peas on high for 3 minutes (or boil for 3 minutes in a small pan with boiling water to cover, then drain) and add to the cooked mushrooms.

5 Cook the noodles in a large saucepan of boiling water for 4–5 minutes until soft yet chewy or slightly elastic. Immediately drain through a sieve and rinse thoroughly under running warm water. Be sure not to overcook the noodles or they will lose their texture. If you like, cut the noodles with scissors into shorter pieces for easier eating. Transfer the noodles to a serving platter or dish and top with the sauce, mushrooms and peas. Serve immediately.

Boerewors (pronounced bore-eh-vors) is a South African sausage that is usually cooked on a *braai* or barbecue. Normally eaten in a roll (like a hot dog) and topped with a tomato and onion relish, it's a delicious and easy way to entertain friends and family on a hot summer's day. Here in the UK, boerewors can be found, at a price, in some butchers or in South African speciality shops; however, it's so easy to make up meatballs at home using the same boerewors spices. Serve them with tomato and onions over hot cauliflower mash and eat them in front of a lovely warm log fire.

BOEREWORS MEATBALLS WITH TOMATO AND ONION RELISH

DAIRY-FREE/GLUTEN-FREE/KETO/PALEO

SERVES 4–6

500g pork mince

500g beef mince

1 egg

2 tbsp raw apple cider vinegar

1 tbsp ground coriander

1 tsp freshly grated nutmeg

½ tsp ground allspice

½ tsp ground cumin

1 tsp garlic granules

1 tsp onion granules

1 tsp pink salt

cauli mash (page 72), to serve

FOR THE TOMATO AND ONION RELISH

1 tbsp avocado oil

1–2 onions, to taste, sliced

3 tomatoes, sliced

1 tbsp dried Italian herbs

1 tsp pink salt

chilli flakes, to taste (optional)

1 tbsp raw apple cider vinegar

1 Preheat the oven to 200°C (180°C fan oven) Gas 6. Line a baking tray with baking paper. In a large bowl combine both minces, the egg, vinegar, spices and flavourings, and mix together using your hands.

2 Roll the meat into balls about the size of golf balls, and put them on the prepared baking tray, leaving a small space between each. Cook in the oven for 30 minutes.

3 Meanwhile, crack on with the relish. Heat the oil in a frying pan over a medium-high heat and cook the onions and tomatoes for 5 minutes or until softened.

4 Reduce the heat to low and add the flavourings and vinegar. Cook over a low heat until the meatballs are ready to be served. Have a taste and add more flavour to the sauce if necessary (a touch of chilli is also great).

5 Serve the meatballs with cauli mash, topped with the tomato and onion relish.

I call these Hercules burgers because they are just an all-round big burger: big on flavour and size. Homemade burgers are always such a treat, and the best part is you are in control of exactly how big you want the burger patty to be. As we don't eat our burgers with a bun but rather use lettuce cups, I like the patty to be bigger and more generous. Add any extra toppings of your choice (or whatever is in the fridge) and serve with a side of Parsnip Fries (page 140) to make the perfect burger-and-fries night in.

HERCULES BURGERS

DAIRY-FREE/GLUTEN-FREE/KETO/PALEO

MAKES 4–6

500g beef mince

½ onion, finely chopped

1 tsp dried parsley

½ tsp garlic powder

½ tsp pink salt

¼ tsp ground black pepper

½ tsp paprika

2 tbsp coconut aminos or Worcestershire Sauce (page 155)

1–2 tbsp avocado oil, as needed, for frying and for greasing

1–2 iceberg lettuces, as needed, to serve

Parsnip Fries (page 140) and toppings of choice, to serve (see Tip)

1 Combine all the ingredients and mix well. Divide the meat into four to six portions. I like to use a metal measuring cup greased with oil to shape them, then I firmly press a portion of meat into the cup. Run a knife around the edge and give the cup a hard bang on a board to produce a perfectly cut patty.

2 Heat a frying pan with the oil and fry the patties on each side for 4–5 minutes for rare to medium, or longer depending on how well done you like your meat. Leave to rest and keep warm while you prepare the toppings.

3 To make the lettuce cups, cut a 10cm chunk from either side of the lettuce, then separate then leaves to create a shell or 'bun'. I can usually get about three 'buns' from one lettuce. Save the remaining lettuce for a salad. Serve the burgers with fries and your favourite toppings.

TIP

Top the burgers with fried onions, sliced avocado, tomato slices, mayonnaise and ketchup.

TRY SOMETHING DIFFERENT

Use crab meat as an alternative to the beef. It is really important to squeeze any excess liquid out of the crab meat before mixing. Follow the same ingredients and simply add 2 beaten eggs and 2 tbsp coconut flour to the mixture, then cook for 5 minutes per side until golden.

My girls love loaded sweet potato wedges, and they are a fun and great way to get vegetables into fussy eaters without them even knowing. If you are a bean-loving family, feel free to add a tin of red kidney beans, or use them as an alternative to meat for a vegan meal. If you are feeding little ones, obviously hold back on the chilli – this is a hot and spicy one!

BEEF CHILLI-LOADED SWEET POTATO WEDGES

DAIRY-FREE/GLUTEN-FREE/PALEO

SERVES 4-6

1 tbsp avocado oil

1 small onion, chopped

½ red pepper, seeded and chopped

½ yellow pepper, seeded and chopped

½ orange pepper, seeded and chopped

2–3 garlic cloves, to taste, crushed

500g minced beef

400g tin chopped tomatoes

2 tbsp tomato purée

1 tbsp red wine vinegar

2 tsp paprika

1–2 tsp chilli flakes, to taste

1 tsp ground cumin

1 tsp ground oregano

coconut yogurt, sliced chilli and Kombucha Pickled Red Onion (page 159) to serve

1 Preheat the oven to 200°C (180°C fan oven) Gas 6. Line a baking tray with baking paper. To make the potato wedges, put the sweet potatoes in a bowl and add the oil and salt. Toss or mix well, then turn onto the prepared baking tray. Roast for 30 minutes or until crispy on the outside and soft inside.

2 Meanwhile, heat the oil in a frying pan over a medium-high heat and cook the onion and peppers for 5–7 minutes or until softened.

3 Add the garlic and beef, then cook until brown. Add the remaining ingredients, reduce the heat to medium and leave to cook gently until the potatoes are ready. Add a splash of water if needed.

4 Once the potatoes have finished roasting, serve them with the chilli and with coconut yogurt, sliced chilli and pickled red onions (page 159).

FOR THE POTATO WEDGES

2–3 medium sweet potatoes, as needed, unpeeled and cut into wedges

2 tbsp avocado oil

1 tsp pink salt

VEGAN ALTERNATIVE

Make it vegan by substituting the beef for 400g tin lentils and 400g tin kidney beans, drained and rinsed.

TIP

For a rich and flavoursome mince, cook for longer at a lower heat.

Dressing the board is a great way to serve a steak. Basically, you fry the steak (or grill it on the barbecue), and while the steak is cooking, you season a wooden chopping board so that when the steak is ready it is then coated in an avocado oil, herb and spice mixture and left to rest on the board or in a serving dish. When you slice into the meat, all those gorgeous flavours are incorporated – and what you end up with is pretty-much steak nirvana.

BAVETTE STEAK IN HERBS AND OIL

DAIRY-FREE/GLUTEN-FREE/KETO/PALEO

SERVES 4–6

1kg bavette/flank steak

1 tbsp avocado oil

pink salt and ground black pepper

FOR THE BOARD DRESSING

60ml avocado oil

juice of 2 lemons, or 2 tbsp balsamic vinegar

a handful of fresh mixed herbs, such as parsley, coriander, rosemary, sage, finely chopped

1 tsp pink salt

1 tsp garlic granules

½ tsp paprika or chilli powder

1 Lightly season the steak with salt and pepper. Heat the oil in a large skillet or griddle over a high heat until it's searing hot.

2 Meanwhile, prepare a large wooden carving board (with grooves around the edge to collect the juices) or a roasting tin by mixing together the oil, lemon juice, herbs and flavourings on the board.

3 Put the steak in the hot pan and sear for 2 minutes. Turn it over and cook for a further 2 minutes or until it reaches your desired doneness – turn the steak only once (see Tip).

4 Remove the steak from the pan and leave it to rest on the board (or serving dish) in the herby oil for at least 5 minutes, although 10 minutes is better. Slice and serve as is on the board.

TIP

If you use a meat thermometer it will tell you when the desired doneness is reached:

Rare: 48ºC

Medium rare: 52ºC

Medium: 55ºC

Don't cook bavette steak past medium, or it will become tough.

VEGAN ALTERNATIVE

Make it vegan by using slices of aubergine cooked in the same way.

TRY SOMETHING DIFFERENT

Substitute with fresh tuna steaks for a delicious fish alternative.

The idea to roast in kombucha came to me many years ago when I needed a healthier way to cook my Christmas gammon. Traditionally, I would boil it in a saucepan full of ginger beer, but when our diets changed, I needed to make an alternative plan. I came up with the idea of using ginger kombucha instead.

Kombucha is difficult to make at home, so I leave it to the experts and purchase it from my supermarket. These days it's available in most of the bigger stores, and in fact over the past few years the selection has grown to a variety of different brands and exciting flavours. I still stick to buying a ginger flavour when making these ribs, but feel free to play around with different flavours.

KOMBUCHA AND MISO-ROASTED SPARE RIBS

DAIRY-FREE/GLUTEN-FREE/KETO/PALEO

SERVES 4-6

4 racks of baby back pork ribs

pink salt and ground black pepper

700ml ginger kombucha

FOR THE MISO BASTING

4 tbsp brown rice miso paste

2 tbsp raw honey, or maple syrup or sweetener

4 tbsp coconut aminos

2 tsp sriracha or chilli sauce

1 Preheat the oven to 180°C (160°C fan oven) Gas 4. Prepare and line a roasting tin with foil (if your oven is small you might need two tins). Clean the ribs by trimming any visible fat and try to remove the thin membrane that runs along the inside of the ribs. Season the ribs with salt and pepper, then put them meat-side up in the prepared tin and pour in the kombucha.

2 Cover and seal the meat with another layer of foil to create a sealed envelope. Bake for 3 hours.

3 Make the miso basting by combining the ingredients in a bowl, then set it aside. Wait for the ribs to come out of the oven, then use 4 tablespoons of the pork juices to thin the basting to a pourable consistency. Discard the remaining kombucha from the tin. Preheat the grill.

4 Baste the ribs on both sides using all the basting mixture, then grill them for a few minutes on either side the sauce is bubbling and browned. Serve.

TIP

These can be made in a fraction of the time using an Instant Pot or an electric pressure cooker. Simply put the ribs in the Instant Pot, use only 330ml of kombucha, then cook on high pressure for 25 minutes. Remove, then baste and grill as above.

I can't say that I'm a massive anchovy fan, but I do love the salty flavour in this sauce when it's teamed up with a delicious roast lamb fillet. Years ago I watched with both fascination and hesitation as my friend Meg made up a marinade for a roast leg of lamb using anchovies; needless to say it was a huge success and I loved the concept. I've paired up anchovies with lamb in so many different ways since. Not only do they add a gorgeous umami flavour but they also add a healthy powerful punch of vitamins and nutrients. Start preparations the day before.

LAMB NECK FILLETS WITH MINT UMAMI SAUCE

DAIRY-FREE/GLUTEN-FREE/KETO/PALEO

SERVES 4

100g fresh mint leaves

25g flat-leaf parsley

100g jar of anchovies in olive oil

2 tbsp capers

120ml olive oil, plus extra for frying

1 garlic clove, crushed

4 lamb neck fillets

TIP

This can be served either warm or cooled.

1 Put the mint in a blender and add the parsley, anchovies, capers, olive oil and crushed garlic. Blend together.

2 Put two-thirds of the mixture in a zip storage bag or dish and add the lamb fillets. Leave the lamb to marinate in the fridge for as long as possible, ideally overnight. Save the remaining mixture in the fridge to serve later as a side sauce.

3 Heat the oven grill (to medium if possible). Heat an ovenproof frying pan over high heat with a drizzle of oil. Remove the lamb from the marinade.

4 Sear the lamb fillets on all sides, one at a time. Put all the fillets back into the pan, or in a roasting tin, and grill for 5 minutes on each side.

5 Remove the lamb from the grill, leave to rest for 5 minutes, then slice and serve with the remaining mint sauce on the side.

Chicken liver is one of those ingredients we either love or hate, but offal is so important to consume in a healthy diet, and liver is probably one of the most nutrient-dense foods on the planet. Serve these creamy, spicy livers with slices of toasted Olive Oil Keto Bread (page 192) and a big green salad and, trust me, they will be a hit at any dinner table.

CREAMY SPICY CHICKEN LIVERS

DAIRY-FREE/GLUTEN-FREE/KETO/PALEO

SERVES 4

500g organic chicken livers (definitely pay up and buy organic)

1 tbsp avocado oil

1 small onion, sliced

1 tsp garlic granules

½ tsp paprika

1 tsp pink salt

1 tsp dried oregano

½ tsp chilli flakes (optional)

160ml coconut cream

2 tbsp tomato purée

2 tbsp homemade Worcestershire Sauce (page 155)

1 tbsp lemon juice

2 tbsp brandy (optional)

fresh herbs, such as parsley, thyme, to garnish

chunky toasted Olive Oil Keto Bread (page 192) or mini lettuce cups, to serve

TIP

For a vegan alternative, substitute the livers for chopped oyster mushrooms.

1 Trim the livers of any excess fat and cut them into bite-sized pieces. Heat the oil in a frying pan over a medium-high heat and cook the onion until soft and starting to turn brown.

2 Add the livers and cook until the outside is browned.

3 Add the remaining ingredients, except for the brandy, if using, reduce the heat and allow the livers to simmer gently for 5–8 minutes until cooked, but the liver should be slightly pink in the middle.

4 Stir in the brandy. Top with the herbs and serve from the pan with a slice of chunky toasted olive oil bread or in mini lettuce cups.

I'd love to say that this recipe was inspired by a trip to Morocco, but sadly not. Perhaps one day I'll get to travel to Morocco to experience first hand the incredible colours and flavours of Moroccan cuisine. In the meantime, I'm bringing Morocco to you in your kitchen.

MOROCCAN ROAST CHICKEN

DAIRY-FREE/GLUTEN-FREE/KETO/PALEO

SERVES 4–6

2 tbsp avocado oil

1 lemon, halved

a handful of fresh thyme sprigs

1.5kg free-range chicken

3 large onions, thickly sliced

FOR THE MOROCCAN SPICES

1 tsp onion granules

1 tsp garlic granules

1 tsp ground cumin

1 tsp ground ginger

1 tsp pink salt

½ tsp ground black pepper

½ tsp ground cinnamon

½ tsp ground coriander

½ tsp cayenne pepper

½ tsp ground allspice

¼ tsp ground cloves

TIP

If the spices start to burn, lightly cover the top of the chicken with a piece of foil.

1 Preheat the oven to 200°C (180°C fan oven) Gas 6. In a small bowl mix all the Moroccan spices together, then mix in the oil.

2 Push the lemon halves and thyme into the cavity of the chicken.

3 Brush the spice oil over the entire chicken, top and bottom.

4 Spread the onion slices over the base of an ovenproof dish and put the chicken on top of the onions. Roast for 20 minutes, then reduce the heat to 180°C (160°C fan oven) Gas 4 for a further 1 hour. Take the chicken out of the oven and leave it to rest for 10 minutes.

5 Carve the chicken and return it to the roasting dish to serve with the onions and juices.

This dish is probably cooked the most frequently in our house out of all my recipes. It is just so simple, and I generally find that I always have chicken pieces in the freezer and lemons in my fruit bowl. Served with a simple green salad and Parsnip Fries (page 142), it makes for a really tasty yet easy meal.

LEMON ROASTED CHICKEN

DAIRY-FREE/GLUTEN-FREE/KETO/PALEO

SERVES 4–6

1kg chicken drumsticks and thighs

2 lemons, quartered

1 tsp pink salt

1 tsp garlic granules

1 tsp Italian herbs

TRY SOMETHING DIFFERENT

To level up this dish, add a whole head of fresh garlic, cut horizontally through the middle into two halves, to the roasting dish and roast. Squeeze out the baked garlic and serve with the chicken.

Substitute the chicken with cod pieces and bake at 200°C (180°C fan oven) Gas 6 for 10–15 minutes depending on the thickness. You want the fish to flake easily when cooked.

1 Preheat the oven to 220°C (200°C fan oven) Gas 7. Lay the chicken pieces in a baking dish, then add the lemons dotted around between the chicken legs.

2 Sprinkle the salt, garlic granules and herbs evenly over the chicken. Roast for 40 minutes or until the skin on the chicken looks crispy (it might even look a tad dry, but don't worry).

3 Using two spoons, squeeze the baked lemons over the chicken and spoon over some of the chicken juices. Return to the oven and bake for a further 10 minutes or until crispy. Serve.

For years, I avoided cooking Asian-style dishes. I'm not exactly sure why, because, to be fair, it is one of the quickest, easiest and most satisfying ways to cook a tasty, healthy meal. It's about frying the ingredients really fast and adding a whack of big flavour combinations. Getting the combinations correct is key, and once you've nailed that, variations of this dish will fast become your go-to for a quick, tasty and nutritious family meal.

CHICKEN FRIED RICE

DAIRY-FREE/GLUTEN-FREE/KETO/PALEO

SERVES 4–6

4 tbsp avocado oil

1 onion, chopped

2 garlic cloves, crushed

500g skinless boneless chicken thighs

125ml coconut aminos

a thumb-sized piece of fresh ginger, peeled and finely grated

½ tsp ground black pepper

1 tsp fish sauce

1 tbsp sesame oil

2 tbsp sesame seeds

1 spring onion, sliced

2 free-range eggs

1 tbsp avocado oil

Cashew Cauli-Rice (page 134)

1 Heat 3 tbsp of the oil in a large frying pan over a medium-high heat and cook the onion for 8 minutes or until soft and translucent.

2 Add the garlic and fry for a few seconds, then add the chicken and mix well. Fry the chicken until it starts to turn brown and crispy.

3 In a small bowl, mix together the aminos, grated ginger, black pepper and fish sauce.

4 Pour the mixture over the browned chicken. Reduce the heat to medium and cook until the chicken is cooked all the way through and the sauce has reduced by half and thickened to become deliciously sticky.

5 Remove from the heat, drizzle sesame oil over and sprinkle with the sesame seeds and sliced spring onion.

6 In a separate pan, fry the eggs in the remaining 1 tbsp oil, breaking the egg yolks. Chop the cooked eggs into small pieces and stir through the Cashew Cauli-Rice. Serve with the chicken.

TRY SOMETHING DIFFERENT

Feel free to add a selection of vegetables such as sugar-snap peas, broccoli, baby corn or peppers. For variety, change the protein to thin slices of beef, pork, firm white fish, salmon or prawns, or for a vegan alternative use oyster or king mushrooms and omit the eggs.

The perfect tenders must be a combination of crunchy on the outside, and soft and tender inside; and most importantly the crumb must pack a load of flavour. Just because we follow a predominantly grain-free diet, doesn't mean that we can't enjoy the comforts of delicious, well-cooked crumbed chicken.

Although this recipe might take time to make because the chicken should ideally spend a night resting in coconut kefir, if you are pushed for time, even an hour's marinating will do. Another essential part to this recipe that should definitely not be skipped is roasting the crumbs before coating the chicken.

CRUMBED CHICKEN TENDERS

DAIRY-FREE/GLUTEN-FREE/KETO/PALEO

SERVES 4

400g mini chicken breast fillets (or regular breasts cut into slices the size of a finger)

400ml coconut kefir or 400ml tinned full-fat coconut milk and 2 tbsp raw apple cider vinegar

1 tbsp pink salt

mayonnaise (with oysters or plain, page 163), for dipping

FOR THE CRUMB

100g almond flour

50g desiccated coconut

1 tsp pink salt

1 tsp onion granules

2 tsp garlic granules

1 tsp dried parsley

1 tsp dried oregano

1 tsp mustard powder

1 tsp paprika

2 free-range eggs

1 Start the night before if possible. Put the chicken in a dish and add the kefir and salt. Leave overnight (or for as long as possible if marinating on the day of cooking).

2 Preheat the grill. Line a baking tray with baking paper. Put the crumb ingredients, except for the eggs, on the paper and mix well together. Spread them out, then put the tray under the grill for 1–2 minutes until crispy and brown, stirring once or twice (keep watching them, because they brown very quickly).

3 Remove the crumbs and transfer them to a plate. Keep the lined baking tray for cooking the chicken. Preheat the oven to 200°C (180°C fan oven) Gas 6.

4 Beat the eggs in a shallow bowl and put it with the plate of crumbs to form a production line. (I find it best to have everything in a row ready to go, with each bowl using a separate fork, otherwise everything becomes clogged up.) Start with the egg, then the crumb, then the baking tray.

5 Using a fork, lift a piece of chicken from the marinade, dunk it in the egg, covering it entirely, then into the crumb, then put it on the paper. Continue until all the chicken is coated.

6 Leave space between each chicken piece to ensure that they become crispy; if the tray is crowded, they won't crisp. Bake for 30 minutes. Serve immediately with a small bowl of mayo for dipping.

This pie is inspired by Tracy, my best friend and an amazing home cook (although she always argues this). When we lived in Cape Town, she would make an incredible chicken pie for our ladies' book club that made me quietly wish that she would host it all the time. The thing about hosting a book club is that you want a dish that is easy enough to prepare, and even easier to serve, yet it has all the ladies oohing and asking for the recipe. Her secret to saving time and adding heaps of flavour was to use a fresh roasted rotisserie chicken from the local supermarket – genius I'd say!

This crust is not your regular-style crust, in that you really don't need patisserie skills or pastry knowledge to make it. Instead of covering the pie in one big sheet, break it up into pieces almost as you would a puzzle or patchwork, which will give you a crunchy pastry topping.

CHICKEN, MUSHROOM AND LEEK PIE

DAIRY-FREE/GLUTEN-FREE/KETO/PALEO

SERVES 4-6

1 rotisserie chicken

1 tbsp avocado oil

2 leeks, sliced

200g button mushrooms, halved or sliced if necessary

1 garlic clove, crushed

400g full-fat canned coconut milk

2 tsp arrowroot powder

4 tbsp brown rice miso paste

150g frozen peas

FOR THE CRUST

250g almond flour

4 tbsp coconut flour

2 tsp gluten-free baking powder

½ tsp pink salt

2 free-range eggs, beaten, plus 1 extra beaten egg, to glaze

125ml coconut kefir or nut milk

chopped parsley, to garnish

green salad, to serve

1 Preheat the oven to 180°C (160°C fan oven) Gas 4. Tear apart the roasted chicken, caveman-style, removing all the meat from the bones. Dig out as much of the meat as possible from all the little nooks and crannies. Chop up the larger chunks into bite-sized pieces and cut the skin into small pieces.

2 Heat the oil in a frying pan over a medium-high heat and fry the leeks and mushrooms and garlic for 5 minutes or until soft. Transfer to a large pie dish, and separate the leek slices once cooled.

3 In the same pan heat the coconut milk and whisk through the arrowroot powder, then stir in the miso paste. Pour this over the leeks and mushrooms.

(continued over page)

4 Add the peas and chicken pieces to the dish and mix everything together, ensuring that the sauce covers all the chicken pieces, then set aside and start with the crust.

5 To make the crust, sift the almond flour, coconut flour, baking powder and salt into a bowl.

6 Make a well in the centre and add the 2 eggs and the kefir. Mix together with a fork or with your hands.

7 Transfer the dough to a silicon mat or a sheet of baking paper and cover with another sheet of baking paper. Roll it out to the approximate size of the pie dish. Break or cut the dough into smaller, more manageable pieces and gently lift the individual pieces of the dough onto the baking dish. Create a patchwork kind of crust by placing pieces together on top of the chicken filling.

8 Brush with a beaten egg, then bake for 30 minutes or until the crust is a gorgeous golden brown. Garnish with a sprinkle of chopped parsley and serve with a green salad.

TRY SOMETHING DIFFERENT.

Turn this dish into a fish pie by substituting the roast chicken with 750g fish pie mixture (usually salmon, cod and haddock, which is available in the fish sections on your supermarket – or chat to your fishmonger). Pat the fish pieces dry with kitchen paper then add them to the pan of cooked onion, leeks and garlic. Gently stir over the heat for a further 3 minutes, then continue as per the above recipe.

Somewhere along the way, many years ago, a tradition started in our house to have pizzas on Friday nights. We started out with the original: the easy local delivery. Or was it? It turns out that they always took so long to deliver on busy Friday nights – and, yes, apparently 'hangry' is a thing!

Over the years our pizza bases have changed and evolved in line with our different diets (my guys are very glad I'm over the cauliflower phase). This base, however, has become our firm favourite, as it is gluten- and dairy-free, vegan and keto, so all of us can enjoy and share the same pizza.

You can make the dough a few days before and store it in the fridge in an airtight container, or bake the bases and freeze them for an easy, quick Friday-night dinner.

FRIDAY NIGHT PIZZA

DAIRY-FREE/GLUTEN-FREE/KETO/PALEO

SERVES 1–2

For the base:

1 tsp raw honey

1 packet fast-action/ easy-bake yeast

60g coconut flour

30g almond flour

2 tbsp psyllium husk

½ tsp pink salt

60ml avocado oil

1 tsp raw apple cider vinegar

FOR THE TOMATO SAUCE

160g tomato passata

35g tomato purée

1 tbsp raw apple cider vinegar

½ tsp pink salt

1 tsp garlic granules

1 Preheat the oven to 220°C (200°C fan oven) Gas 7. To make the base, put 250ml warm water (45°C to be precise) in a bowl and add the honey and yeast. (If you have a thermometer, it's best to use it for the water, as the correct temperature is important to activate the yeast; but if you don't, the temperature of warm bath water is good.) Mix together.

2 Set it aside for 10 minutes to activate. Put the coconut flour in a food processor and add the almond flour, psyllium husk and salt, then blitz to mix well.

3 Once the yeast has started to activate (it should be foamy and strong smelling) pour it into the dry ingredients and add the oil and vinegar. Blitz for a few seconds, then scrape down the sides and blitz again.

4 Transfer the batter to a sheet of baking paper and knead it into a ball. The batter will be different from regular batter: it might feel a little crumbly, but it will still hold its shape.

(continued over page)

1 tsp paprika

1 tsp Italian herbs

2 tsp raw honey, or maple syrup or sweetener

FOR THE DAIRY-FREE PARMESAN CHEESE

50g flaked almonds

20g nutritional yeast flakes

½ tsp pink salt

½ tsp garlic granules

FOR THE TOPPINGS

Choose from a variety of toppings (ours are usually what is on hand in the fridge), such as bacon, chicken, ham, fresh tomatoes, basil or rocket, grilled onions or slices of red onions, a variety of peppers and, of course, fresh chopped chilli

TIP

Store any Parmesan leftovers in an airtight container and use over salads, pizzas or noodles.

5 Flatten the ball and top with another sheet of baking paper, then, using a rolling pin, roll from the centre out to form a large circle.

6 Shape and neaten the edges, then fold or roll them back in on themselves by about 2.5cm to create a thick crust edge, the way you want it to look when baked.

7 Transfer to a baking sheet. Bake for 10 minutes, then remove from the oven. (At this point you can leave it to cool for later if you wish.)

8 Meanwhile, to make the sauce, put all the ingredients in a saucepan over a medium heat and heat through until hot and bubbling. (Alternatively, use a microwave.)

9 To make the dairy-free Parmesan cheese, blitz the ingredients together in a food processor.

10 Spoon the sauce onto the cooked pizza base. Add your chosen toppings and sprinkle with the dairy-free Parmesan. Put the pizza back in the oven for a further 10 minutes or until cooked through. Serve.

I only started to eat prawns as an adult, and even more recently learned to cook them; all those years wasted – such a pity! I guess I had always been put off by the thought of cleaning and peeling them. Although I realise that fresh is best, frozen prawns are just incredibly convenient, and now I always have a bag of frozen prawns for an emergency meal. Defrosting is simple, just pop them in a bowl of warm water and they defrost in a few minutes and are then ready to use in my quick and easy prawn stew.

PRAWN STEW

DAIRY-FREE/GLUTEN-FREE/KETO/PALEO

SERVES 4

2 tbsp avocado oil

1 onion, chopped

1 leek, sliced

1 red pepper, seeded and sliced

2–3 garlic cloves, to taste, crushed

400g cauliflower florets

400g broccoli florets

350ml tinned coconut cream

1 tbsp tomato purée

1 tbsp harissa paste

1 tsp pink salt

400g shelled prawns

4 tbsp chopped fresh dill, plus extra to serve

1 Heat the oil in a large saucepan over a medium-high heat and cook the onion, leek, pepper and garlic for 5 minutes or until soft.

2 Meanwhile, steam the cauliflower and broccoli florets.

3 Add the coconut cream to the onion mixture followed by the tomato purée, harissa paste and salt, and stir to mix well.

4 Once the cream starts to boil, add the prawns and stir through, ensuring that they are covered with the sauce. Leave to cook for a few minutes until they turn a pale pink colour (cooking time will depend on their size).

5 Stir through the chopped dill. Serve warm over the steamed broccoli and cauliflower with a sprinkle of dill.

Cooking salmon could not get any easier than this, and it's such a crowd pleaser to serve either to your family or at a dinner party. All you're doing is simply covering the salmon in pesto and baking it – there's nothing else to it. The trick comes in making sure that you have a jar of homemade pesto waiting patiently in the fridge. Not to chest beat, but I always have one in mine because Kyra eats it on everything – and I mean *everything*! If you don't have a jar hanging around, store-bought will also work well.

BAKED SALMON WITH PESTO

DAIRY-FREE/GLUTEN-FREE/KETO/PALEO

SERVES 4–6

1kg fresh whole salmon fillet or salmon pieces

125ml Pesto (page 156)

chopped dill, to garnish

Kombucha Pickled Red Onion (page 159) and edible flowers, to serve (optional)

1 Preheat the oven to 180°C (160°C fan oven) Gas 4. Line a baking tray with foil then with a sheet of baking paper, and put the salmon skin-side down on the paper.

2 Thickly spread over the pesto, covering the entire top of the fillet. Bake for 30 minutes or until the flesh flakes easily.

3 Garnish with dill and topped with pickled red onion and few edible flowers if you are feeling fancy.

The Daily Catch

Fish & Chips   35p

Using pork scratching as a crumb is truly one of the tastiest grain-free (and high-protein) ways to crumb food. I buy my pork scratching from the gluten-free aisle or the crisps section of my local supermarkets. Take time to read the packet, ensuring that it's gluten-free and quality-raised pork. I usually keep a few packets in my pantry for a last-minute crumb that can be thrown on any kind of protein or over a veg to add a gorgeous crunch.

FISH GOUJONS

DAIRY-FREE/GLUTEN-FREE/KETO/PALEO

SERVES 4–6

800g cod or hake fillet, skinned

200g gluten-free pork scratching (about 5 regular-sized packets, I use Awfully Posh)

50g cassava flour

1 tsp pink salt

1 tsp chilli powder (optional)

1 egg

Oyster Mayonnaise (page 163), to serve

1 Preheat the oven to 220°C (200°C fan oven) Gas 7. Line a baking tray with baking paper. Slice the fish into 3cm (1¼in) wide pieces.

2 Empty the packets of scratching into a food processor and blitz to a crumb, then transfer to a plate.

3 Mix the flour, salt and chilli together on a separate plate to the crumb. Whisk the egg in a shallow bowl. Make a production line starting with the flour, egg, crumb and then the baking tray.

4 Using a clean fork in each dish, start by dunking the fish in the flour and covering it entirely, then into the egg, then firmly pressing it into the crumb on both sides, then line them up on the baking paper, ensuring that you leave a space between each piece.

5 Bake for 10 minutes, then turn on the grill and cook for 3–5 minutes until crispy, golden and crunchy. Serve immediately with oyster mayo.

I prefer to make this recipe using canned pumpkin, because that way I can ensure that it's the same consistency and texture every time. Depending on the time of year, pumpkins differ in texture, and this recipe won't work if the pumpkin is very watery, so using canned pumpkin is a safe option. I find my canned pumpkin in the American or baking sections of my supermarket or from Amazon.

PUMPKIN GNOCCHI

DAIRY-FREE/GLUTEN-FREE/PALEO/VEGAN

SERVES 4

425g canned pumpkin purée (or fresh, cooked, see above)

100g cassava flour, sifted

2 tbsp coconut flour, sifted, plus extra if needed

pink salt

½ tsp garlic powder

avocado oil, for frying

1 large red onion, sliced

100g raw walnuts, crushed

1–2 tbsp Pesto (page 156), to taste, to serve

TRY SOMETHING DIFFERENT

Take this dish to a whole new level by adding anchovy fillets for a punch of flavour, healthy oils and protein.

TIP

If you prefer to use fresh homemade pumpkin purée, cut a pumpkin into wedges and roast at 220°C (200°C fan oven) Gas 7 until soft, golden and crispy on the outside (it should be mashable with a fork), allowing them to dry out as much as possible. Scoop out the flesh, purée it and weigh out 425g. You might need to add an extra 1–2 tbsp coconut flour to get it to the playdough consistency.

1 Fill a saucepan halfway with boiling water and add a sprinkle of salt, then return it to the boil.

2 Mix together the pumpkin purée, cassava flour, coconut flour, ½ tsp pink salt and the garlic powder. It should be a play dough consistency; if not, mix in an extra 1–2 tsp coconut flour.

3 Roll the batter into three logs on baking paper. Cut individual pieces about 3cm long and press them down slightly with a wet fork to leave an indentation. Transfer them in batches to the boiling water.

4 When they rise to the top of the water, remove them with a slotted spoon and put them on a plate lined with kitchen paper. Continue until all the dough is finished.

5 Heat the oil in a non-stick frying pan over a medium-high heat.

6 Fry the gnocchi in batches (don't worry if they leave a crispy layer in the pan).

7 Remove the fried gnocchi and add more oil to fry the onion, scraping up any of the crispy layers left behind from the gnocchi.

8 Add the crushed walnuts and heat them through, then return the gnocchi to the pan and heat through. Serve with a dollop of pesto.

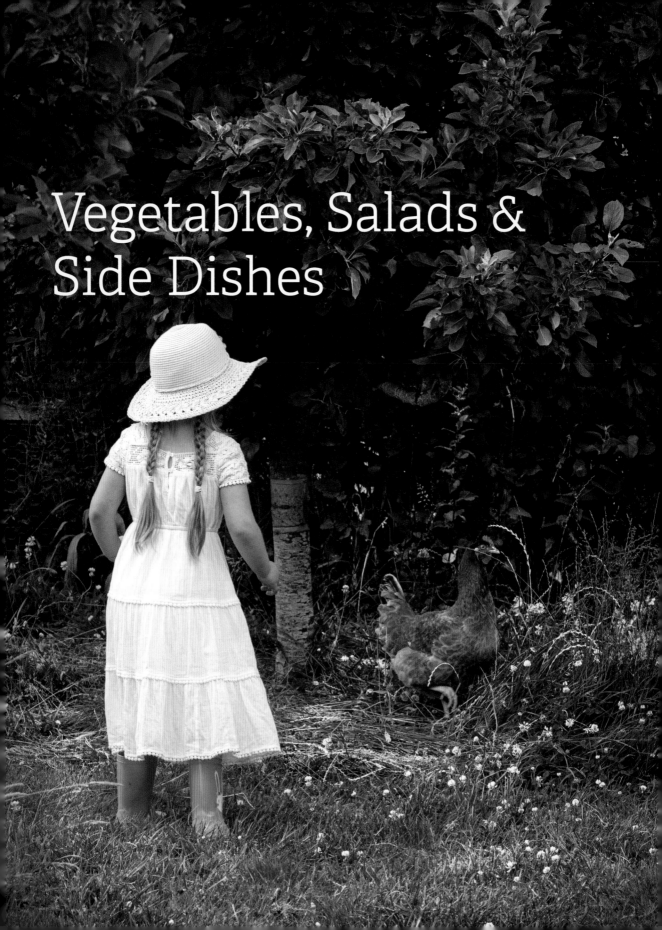

Vegetables, Salads &
Side Dishes

As much as I adore coleslaw and would pretty much eat it with anything, I've noticed that so many people wrinkle their nose up at the mention of it, which got me thinking about how I could create a new and exciting version. This dressing is to die for, and it can also be used over rice or sweet potato noodles pad-Thai style.

If you're making the coleslaw in advance (which can be done up to a day ahead), be sure to leave the dressing off until just before serving.

THAI RAINBOW COLESLAW

DAIRY-FREE/GLUTEN-FREE/KETO/PALEO/VEGAN

SERVES 4-6

½ red cabbage, thinly sliced

½ sweetheart or green cabbage, thinly sliced

2–3 carrots, as needed, spiralised or cut into ribbons

a big handful of fresh coriander, leaves chopped

1 red chilli, seeded and sliced

2 spring onions, thinly sliced

1–2 tbsp sesame seeds, to taste

1 Put the cabbage in a large bowl and add the carrots, coriander, chilli and spring onions. Toss together.

2 Put all the dressing ingredients in a bowl and mix well, then set aside.

3 Just before serving, drizzle the dressing over the cabbage mixture and sprinkle with sesame seeds.

FOR THE DRESSING

3 tbsp sugar-free peanut butter or nut butter

2 tbsp extra virgin olive oil

60ml coconut aminos

2 tbsp lime juice (from 1 plump lime)

2 tbsp raw apple cider vinegar

2 tbsp sesame oil

½ tsp garlic powder

1–2 tsp chilli flakes, to taste

TIP

Depending on the brand of peanut butter, if the dressing is too thick, simply add a splash of boiling water to thin it out to a pourable consistency.

Last year for Christmas we had both Gemma and her boyfriend Andy needing a vegan roast for lunch. I bought and taste-tested numerous nut roasts and none of them were good enough to be dished up on such a day. Besides not being gluten-free, they were either filled with meat replacements or were just downright tasteless. I decided that a stuffed butternut roast was what I'd make for them and, I'm pleased to say, it was a huge success – in fact, between the two of them, they polished off the whole thing. No surprises, I've been asked to make it again this year!

WALNUT, KALE AND CRANBERRY-STUFFED BUTTERNUT

DAIRY-FREE/GLUTEN-FREE/KETO/PALEO/VEGAN

SERVES 2-4

1 whole butternut, unpeeled

6 garlic cloves, with skin

2 tbsp avocado oil

FOR THE FILLING

3 heaped tbsp dried cranberries

50g (a big handful) fresh kale, stems removed, chopped finely

150g walnuts, crushed

½ tsp pink salt

TIP

Depending on the size of the butternut, cooking times might vary – you want it be soft and scoopable.

1 Preheat the oven to 200°C (180°C fan oven) Gas 6. Cut the butternut in half lengthways.

2 Scoop out the seeds and score the flesh, then pop the garlic cloves into the hollow.

3 Put the squash halves skin-side down in a roasting tin and drizzle with 1 tbsp of the oil.

4 Roast for 50–60 minutes until soft and scoopable, then remove from the oven and leave to cool.

5 Squeeze the garlic cloves from their skins into a bowl and scoop out the flesh of the butternut, leaving a 1cm wall around the edge of the skin. Put the flesh in the bowl.

6 Mash the garlic and butternut together, then stir in the cranberries, kale and walnuts and salt.

7 Return the mixture to both butternut skins and place them together. Tie the butternut together with string and drizzle and rub the skin with the remaining 1 tbsp oil. Bake for a further 30 minutes. Serve sliced.

They say you should eat the colours of the rainbow, and this is the easiest and tastiest way to do it. Don't overthink chopping the vegetables: just chunky chop them, mix them together, then pop them in the oven. It's super-easy and a tasty way to brighten up the dinner table.

EASY GRILLED VEGETABLES

DAIRY-FREE/GLUTEN-FREE/KETO/PALEO/VEGAN

SERVES 4–6

1 red onion, chopped

1 red pepper, seeded and chopped

1 yellow pepper, seeded and chopped

1 orange pepper, seeded and chopped

4–6 baby aubergines or 1 medium, end removed, chopped

2 courgettes, chunky chopped

3 tbsp avocado oil

1 tbsp balsamic glaze

1 tsp pink salt

1 tsp garlic powder or 1 garlic clove, crushed

a handful of fresh chopped mint, to garnish

1 Preheat the oven to 220°C (200°C fan oven) Gas 7. Line a baking tray with baking paper. Put the chopped vegetables in a bowl and toss with the oil, balsamic reduction, salt and garlic.

2 Transfer to the baking tray, making sure to spread the vegetables evenly over the tray, and roast for 25 minutes, stirring or tossing after 15 minutes.

3 Once the timer is up, change the oven to grill and open the door slightly to allow the steam to escape. Grill the vegetables for 5 minutes or until crispy and golden, keeping an eye on them to avoid them burning. Remove from the oven and top with fresh mint before serving.

There is nothing more beautiful than a big bowl of shining colourful tomatoes to entice the family into eating more veggies. The little cherry tomatoes are the tastiest, or, when they're in season, I love to buy heirloom tomatoes, which come in a variety of different sizes and colours, and taste heavenly. A dash of sweetness and some salt really enhances the flavours of this salad beautifully.

TOMATO, OLIVE AND BASIL SALAD

DAIRY-FREE/GLUTEN-FREE/KETO/PALEO

SERVES 6–8

700g mixed cherry tomatoes (the more colours the better), halved

a large handful of basil leaves, chopped

a small handful of mint leaves, chopped

180g pitted kalamata olives, chopped

FOR THE DRESSING

4 tbsp avocado oil

1 tbsp raw honey, or maple syrup or sweetener

1 tbsp raw apple cider vinegar

1 tsp Dijon mustard

1 tsp rock or pink salt

1 Put the tomatoes in a bowl and add the herbs and olives. Mix well.

2 Put the dressing ingredients in a bowl and mix together, then pour over the salad. The longer it stands the tastier the salad gets. This can be made in advance and stored in the fridge for up to a day before serving, although I'd suggest leaving out the fresh herbs until just before serving. Drain the juices if it becomes too watery.

Over the years I have made so many variations of this recipe that it's hard to keep track. It's one of those salads that friends will ask me to bring for a barbecue, because it's not only different and original but it also has such a refreshing and vibrant taste. It's delicious served cold, but it also works beautifully warmed with a meat or veg stew.

The longer it stands the tastier it gets, so make it up well before serving to ensure maximum flavour.

TABBOULEH SALAD

DAIRY-FREE/GLUTEN-FREE/KETO/PALEO/VEGAN

SERVES 4–6

250g broccoli, roughly chopped into chunks

250g cauliflower, roughly chopped into chunks

50g kale, stems removed, chopped

30g fresh mint leaves, finely chopped

30g fresh parsley leaves, finely chopped

juice of 1–2 limes, to taste

80ml extra virgin olive oil

1 tbsp harissa spice powder, or to taste

1 tsp pink salt

100g pomegranate rubies

1 Put the broccoli, cauliflower and kale in a food processor and pulse until they are the size of rice grains (you could also use a grater if you prefer).

2 Put the broccoli, cauliflower and kale in a microwave bowl, cover and microwave on full power for 3 minutes, then remove and leave to cool. (Alternatively, heat through on the hob in a saucepan over a medium heat for 5 minutes, just enough to soften slightly. You could also serve it raw.)

3 Add the mint and parsley to the broccoli mixture, then stir through the remaining ingredients. Taste and add more spice or lime juice if needed. Cover and transfer to the fridge to cool for as long as possible. The flavours intensify the longer they stand, so make life easy and mix this up well in advance.

I love how much excitement there is for British asparagus season in the spring. Growing up I was never really exposed to fresh asparagus, and it was a game-changer when I eventually discovered it – the hype around British asparagus season is worth it!

The wealth of nutrients that seaweed provides is pretty incredible. Seaweed has been an important food source for many cultures for thousands of years, so why not ours? I buy mine from my local farm stall, but it can also be found in health stores and major supermarkets in the Asian section.

ASPARAGUS AND SEAWEED SALAD

DAIRY-FREE/GLUTEN-FREE/KETO/PALEO/VEGAN

SERVES 4

30g dulse, or wakame or kelp

500g fresh asparagus

150g frozen peas

a bunch of fresh mint

4 quail eggs (optional)

1 tbsp avocado oil or olive oil, for egg frying

FOR THE DRESSING

3 tbsp avocado oil or olive oil

3 tbsp fresh lemon juice

3 tbsp coconut kefir or coconut yogurt

¼ tsp dried mustard powder

½ tsp mixed dried herbs

a pinch of rock salt

a pinch of ground black pepper

1 Soak the seaweed in warm water for 5–10 minutes. When soft, remove it and lay it out to dry on kitchen paper.

2 Cut off the ends of the asparagus and, using a paring knife, slice it lengthwise in half.

3 Blanch the asparagus for 2 minutes in a saucepan of boiling water, then remove and leave to cool.

4 Add the frozen peas to the asparagus water and leave for 1 minute then drain them (they don't need to be totally defrosted, as cold peas are really refreshing).

5 Pull some mint leaves off their stem and set them aside until ready to assemble.

6 Using a blender or whisk, combine all the dressing ingredients until smooth.

7 If you are adding eggs, fry them in a frying pan with the oil for 1–2 minutes until cooked yet still soft (they don't take long at all). You could also boil them for 3–5 minutes if you prefer. Assemble the salad and drizzle with the dressing, then serve immediately.

When Kyra was little, she told everyone who would listen that she was highly allergic to salad – well, mainly lettuce. She definitely did not have an allergy to lettuce, however; it was just her way of avoiding eating any form of regular green salad, which is why I had to come up with other forms of salad to fill her plate. Thankfully, she loves broccoli, and when I added a deliciously creamy ranch dressing, she wasn't even aware that she was eating a healthy, filling salad.

BROCCOLI SALAD

DAIRY-FREE/GLUTEN-FREE/KETO/PALEO

SERVES 4–6

4 free-range eggs

5 rashers back bacon, or to taste

600g broccoli, cut into small bite-sized florets

½ red onion, finely chopped

2 tbsp dried cranberries

FOR THE RANCH DRESSING

125ml coconut kefir, or coconut yogurt or coconut cream

80ml mayonnaise (with oysters or plain, page 163)

2 tsp dried parsley

1 tsp garlic powder

1 tsp pink salt

½ tsp dried thyme

1 tsp raw apple cider vinegar

1 Put the eggs in a saucepan of boiling water and return it to the boil. Cook for 10 minutes, then drain the eggs and refill the pan with cold water to cool them. Peel off the shells and chop the eggs. Set aside.

2 Put the bacon in a frying pan over a medium-high heat and fry until crisp. Remove from the pan and set aside.

3 Put the broccoli in a microwave bowl and add 1 tbsp water. Cover and microwave on high for 3–4 minutes until cooked but still firm. Drain the water and leave to cool. (Alternatively, steam the broccoli for 3–4 minutes until cooked but still firm.)

4 Put the broccoli into a salad bowl and add the onion, cranberries, bacon and egg.

5 To make the dressing, put the ingredients in a small bowl and mix together. Pour over the salad and mix well. Leave in the fridge until ready to serve. This salad improves with time, so it can be made 3–4 hours or even a day ahead of serving and left in the fridge.

VEGAN ALTERNATIVE

Make it vegan by leaving out the bacon and eggs. Substitute with vegan mayonnaise or extra coconut cream. Add a sprinkle of mixed seeds and crushed nuts for crunch.

"Having a vegetable garden keeps one young and fit – when your back doesn't fail you! I suppose it's the combination of producing something from the bare earth by your own effort, and that something so much better – fresher, more nourishing, more tasty – than anything you can buy, even from a market stall. It is creative, and as with all creativity there are disappointments and failures, from climate and from marauders such as slugs, birds and rabbits. But to me that is part of what makes growing your own stuff special. There is risk involved. It is between you and nature; sometimes you win, sometimes you lose. It is not like going to the supermarket, where you know you can get anything you want, never mind the quality.

Angela Dyer, aged 80 years

You could save time and make this salad without grilling the courgette, but I personally am not a fan of raw courgette. A mandoline slicer is useful for achieving evenly sliced courgette and radishes, but don't rush out and buy one if you don't already have one lying around at home; just try to ensure that your slices are as thin as possible, carpaccio-style.

GRILLED COURGETTE CARPACCIO SALAD

DAIRY-FREE/GLUTEN-FREE/KETO/PALEO/VEGAN

SERVES 4–6

2 large courgettes, thinly sliced lengthways

200g radishes, thinly sliced

80g pea shoots or watercress

a handful of fresh herbs, such as mint, parsley or coriander, chopped

4 tbsp pomegranate rubies

vegan Parmesan cheese, to serve (optional, see page 102)

FOR THE DRESSING

3 tbsp avocado oil

juice of ½ lemon (about 1 tbsp)

½ tsp dried tarragon

½ tsp dried chilli flakes (optional)

pink salt and ground black pepper

1 The courgette can be left raw if you like. Otherwise, preheat the grill and line a baking tray with baking paper. Put the courgette slices on the prepared baking tray and grill until browned on both sides. Leave to cool, then put the courgette (raw or cooked) into a bowl.

2 To make the dressing, mix the ingredients together in a small bowl. Pour the dressing over the courgette slices and leave to stand for 10 minutes.

3 Toss the other salad ingredients together in a salad bowl, then top with the courgette and dressing and vegan Parmesan cheese. Serve immediately, as it does not last in the fridge.

Aubergine is an incredibly versatile vegetable that is perfect as a vegan meat replacement (bearing in mind that this is only in taste, as it does not match nutrient- or protein-wise). Once cooked, the flesh has a meaty texture without an overbearing flavour, making it ideal to serve either as a side dish or as a main for a meat-free meal.

DRESSED GRILLED AUBERGINE

DAIRY-FREE/GLUTEN-FREE/KETO/PALEO/VEGAN

SERVES 6–8

800g (about 4) aubergines

3 tsp pink or rock salt

3 tbsp avocado oil

1 tsp garlic powder

½ tsp paprika

100g coconut yogurt

100g Pesto (page 156)

10–15 cherry tomatoes, quartered

50g pomegranate rubies

a handful of fresh mint or herbs of choice, leaves chopped

pink salt and ground black pepper

1 Preheat the oven to 200°C (180°C fan oven) Gas 6. Cut the aubergines in half lengthways from top to bottom. Lay them out on a baking tray skin-side down and sprinkle with 2 tsp of the salt.

2 Leave to stand for 10 minutes; you will see little beads of moisture form as the salt extracts the water from the aubergine. Rinse the aubergines, and pat them dry with kitchen paper. Put them on the baking tray.

3 In a small bowl mix together the oil, garlic powder, paprika and the remaining 1 tsp salt. Brush this oil mixture over each aubergine.

4 Bake for 40 minutes or until soft and the flesh can be pulled apart with a fork.

5 Meanwhile, put the coconut yogurt and pesto in a bowl and mix together.

6 In another bowl mix together the chopped tomatoes, pomegranate rubies and chopped herbs, seasoning with salt and pepper if necessary.

7 Remove the aubergines from the oven and leave to cool slightly. Serve with a generous dollop of pesto yogurt and the chopped tomato mixture.

My childhood memory of Brussels sprouts and the ones I make at home these days are two entirely different things. Boiled sprouts at my grandma's table were like sheer torture to my brother Byron and I – we would save them until last, then swallow them whole so that we didn't have to chew them. I know that I'm not the only one with these memories, and I hope that if you are the same, you will give this recipe a go. Who knew that sprouts could be sweet and crunchy when cooked in the correct way?

THE BEST BRUSSELS SPROUTS – EVER!

DAIRY-FREE/GLUTEN-FREE/KETO/PALEO/VEGAN

SERVES 4

500g Brussels sprouts, halved lengthways

2 tbsp avocado oil

pink salt and ground black pepper

FOR THE SAUCE

2 tbsp coconut aminos

1 tbsp sesame oil

¼ tsp garlic granules

¼ tsp chilli powder or smoked paprika

VARIATION

Add a sprinkle of crushed pork scratching for extra crunch, if you like (see Fish Goujons, page 109).

1 Preheat the oven to 250°C (230°C fan oven) Gas 9½ and line a baking tray with baking paper. Put the Brussels sprouts in a bowl and coat with the oil. Season with salt and pepper to taste.

2 Put the sprouts cut-side down on the tray, leaving space between them, then bake for 20 minutes.

3 Mix the sauce ingredients together in a bowl. Drizzle half the sauce over the Brussels, then return them to the oven for 5 minutes, leaving it switched on, but with the door slightly open to allow any steam to escape. Serve immediately with the remaining sauce on the side for dunking.

What are spring greens? Spring greens are the first cabbages of the year, and yes, they differ from other cabbages. They are actually similar to kale in that the central leaves do not form a head, or only a very loose one. They have a soft texture, taste sweeter and fresher and, in my opinion, are tastier than the well-known savoy or January king cabbages, so they fit well with lighter spring and summer cooking: just a flash fry and a squeeze of lemon juice is all that's required for this delicious vegetable.

Most supermarkets in the UK stock chopped packets of spring greens, but if you can't find spring greens on your travels, kale or a pointed spring cabbage will work beautifully as alternatives.

LEMON SPRING GREENS

DAIRY-FREE/GLUTEN-FREE/KETO/PALEO/VEGAN

SERVES 4–6

2 tbsp avocado oil

200g spring greens, sliced into ribbons

1 tsp herbal salt (Herbamare)

25g flaked almonds

juice of 1 lemon, or to taste

1 Heat the oil in a saucepan over medium-high heat. Cook the greens for 3 minutes, turning them over regularly until wilted.

2 Sprinkle with the herbal salt, then transfer them to a serving dish. Serve sprinkled with the flaked almonds and a squeeze of lemon juice to taste.

Although I know cauli-rice is nothing new in the low-carb community, I still find that when I serve it to friends, many have never tasted it before and are really rather impressed by it. The thing about cauli-rice is that it has got to be made correctly to be delicious and satisfying. Replacing a staple such as rice needs to leave your family or guests feeling fully satisfied and not foraging in the fridge an hour later. The addition of cashew nuts is crucial here: they provide the essential fats for satiety and crunch for the rice-like texture. In fact, this cauli-rice is so good that you could even sit down to a bowl of it without anything else on top.

CASHEW CAULI-RICE

DAIRY-FREE/GLUTEN-FREE/KETO/PALEO/VEGAN

SERVES 4

500g cauliflower, cut into even-sized chunks

100g cashew nuts

3 tbsp avocado oil

2 tsp herbal salt (Herbamare), or to taste

TIP

Save the inner cores from cauliflowers when you're cooking, freeze them, then when you have a few on hand, thaw them out and turn them into rice. The core particularly makes a deliciously crunchy rice.

1 Put the cauliflower and cashew nuts in a food processor and blitz until they form rice-sized grains.

2 Heat the oil in a large saucepan over a high heat.

3 Tip the cauli-rice into the pan and shake the pan so that the entire base is covered. Leave for 3 minutes.

4 Using a spatula, gently lift and turn the rice and, again, leave to cook for a further 3 minutes (you can even cover the pan with a lid). Do this a couple of times until the rice starts to look slightly golden and tender. Sprinkle over the herbal salt and mix through, adding more to taste if needed. Serve.

Oh goodness, how I love sweet potato wedges! Way easier than making fries, they really just need to be chopped into chunks and roasted. Leave the skin on for extra nutrition, plus it helps with achieving that beautiful caramelised potato crispness.

SMOKEY SWEET POTATO WEDGES

DAIRY-FREE/GLUTEN-FREE/KETO/PALEO/VEGAN

SERVES 4–6

1 tsp garlic powder

1 tsp paprika

½ tsp chilli powder

1 tsp Italian herbs

1kg (4 large) sweet potatoes, unpeeled, chopped into wedges

60ml avocado oil

1 tsp rock or pink salt

100g pomegranate rubies

a handful of fresh mint or parsley, leaves chopped

FOR THE TAHINI SAUCE

125ml light tahini

60ml fresh lemon juice

a pinch of pink salt

1 tsp harissa paste or powder (optional but adds a really great flavour)

1 Preheat the oven to 200°C (180°C fan oven) Gas 6. Line a baking tray with baking paper. In a small bowl mix together the dry flavourings.

2 Pat the sweet potato wedges dry with kitchen paper, then put in a large bowl, drizzle with the oil, then sprinkle with the dry spices and salt. Rub the wedges to ensure that they are well coated.

3 Transfer to the prepared baking tray and bake for 30 minutes or until cooked through.

4 To make the tahini sauce, put the ingredients in a blender and add 125ml warm water.

5 Blitz together until smooth and creamy. Add more water if needed, as it might become lumpy and dry. Keep blending, and it will magically transform into a gorgeous light and creamy sauce.

6 Turn the oven to grill, and grill the wedges until crisp and beautifully caramelised. You might need to turn them over a few times – keep an eye on them as they can burn quickly.

7 Remove from the oven and serve with a generous drizzle of tahini sauce, pomegranate rubies and fresh herbs.

Salads are not just for summer barbecues with barefoot children running around. There is nothing more delicious than a winter salad served with a bowl of stew or soup. Winter salads are naturally more hearty and filling than their summer counterparts, and they generally include slow-release carbs such as squash and root vegetables. I've included black rice in my winter salad because it has such a deliciously nutty, almost sweet, flavour and it is rich in anthocyanins, which are healthy antioxidant pigments that give the rice its unusual purple-black colour. In traditional Chinese medicine, it's even considered to be a blood tonic – it is certainly good enough to keep your family strong through the winter.

If following a keto diet or low-carb diet, then feel free to replace the rice with cauliflower rice.

WINTER BLACK RICE SALAD

DAIRY-FREE/GLUTEN-FREE/KETO/PALEO/VEGAN

SERVES 4-6

1kg pumpkin or butternut squash, unpeeled, chopped into 2cm thick slices

2 red onions, chunky chopped

1 red pepper, seeded and chunky chopped

1 orange pepper, seeded and chunky chopped

1 yellow pepper, seeded and chunky chopped

2–3 tbsp avocado oil, as needed

1 tbsp ras el hanout, za'atar or harissa spice

1 tsp pink salt

400g black rice

1 Preheat the oven to 180°C (160°C fan oven) Gas 4. Put the pumpkin on a baking tray, and add the onions and peppers. Cover with oil and sprinkle with spice, then bake for 45 minutes or until the pumpkin flesh is soft and the skin is easy to cut and is edible.

2 Fill a saucepan halfway with boiling water and add the salt, then boil the rice for 20 minutes or until soft (it won't be soft like white rice, but rather nutty and with a bite), then drain in a colander and set aside.

3 Mix together the dressing ingredients.

4 Once the pumpkin and vegetables are beautifully roasted, transfer them to a serving platter, then add the rice and mix well.

5 Drizzle the dressing over just before serving, or serve it on the side, and add an extra sprinkle of fresh mint. Serve either hot or cold.

FOR THE DRESSING

125ml coconut kefir or coconut yogurt

30g fresh mint, leaves finely chopped, plus extra to sprinkle

½ tsp pink salt

lemon juice, to taste

TIP

If you can't find black rice, substitute with couscous, quinoa or Cashew Cauli-Rice (page 134).

Parsnips have to be the underdog of the root vegetable world. I bet nobody has ever heard anyone say that parsnips are their favourite vegetable – right? Well, I'm rooting for the underdog, and honestly this way of cooking parsnips as fries will change anyone's opinion. They are as crunchy as potato fries, yet way tastier.

PARSNIP FRIES

DAIRY-FREE/GLUTEN-FREE/KETO/PALEO/VEGAN

SERVES 4–6

1kg parsnips, unpeeled

4 tbsp avocado oil

1 tsp garlic powder

1 tsp pink or rock salt

1 tsp dried tarragon

1 Preheat the oven to 200°C (180°C fan oven) Gas 6. Line a baking tray with baking paper. Chop off both ends of the parsnips then cut them into chip-sized wedges.

2 Put them in a large bowl and cover them with the oil then sprinkle over the garlic powder, salt and tarragon. Mix well to ensure that they are properly covered. Tip into the prepared baking tray and bake for 40 minutes until crisp and golden. Serve.

I'm a sucker for anything creamy and have always loved a creamy sauce for broccoli or cauliflower. In my dairy days I would add a handful of grated cheese to this dish, but a sprinkle of dairy-free Parmesan (see page 102) works beautifully as an alternative. There really is no need to stand around making a full pan of cheese sauce. Hopefully, this will reinvent cheese sauces for you and become something your family loves.

FIVE-MINUTE CREAMY BROCCOLI

DAIRY-FREE/GLUTEN-FREE/KETO/PALEO

SERVES 4

300g broccoli, cut into florets

2 tbsp avocado oil or olive oil

120ml coconut yogurt or coconut cream

2 tbsp mayonnaise (with oysters or plain, see page 163)

3 tbsp dairy-free Parmesan cheese (page 102) or nutritional yeast flakes

1 tsp herbal salt (Herbamare), or to taste

½ tsp dried mustard powder

½ tsp onion granules

TRY SOMETHING DIFFERENT

You could also use cauliflower, although it will require a longer cooking time.

1 Put the broccoli in a microwavable bowl with 3 tbsp water. Cover and microwave on high for 5 minutes or until soft. Remove from the microwave and drain the water. (Alternatively, steam for 5 minutes or until soft and tip into a bowl.)

2 Add the oil and mix well to coat.

3 Put the yogurt in a small bowl and add the mayonnaise, dairy-free Parmesan and flavourings. Mix together well, then pour over the broccoli and combine. Return to the microwave for 1 minute to heat through before serving (or return to the pan without the steamer basket and heat through over a low heat).

We have bid farewell to roast potatoes in our home and welcomed in the cool and hip new pesto-smashed potatoes – which, to be honest, are so incredibly delicious and much easier to make. They are so garlicky, salty and crunchy that my guys would eat them for breakfast if they could – actually, come to think of it, they do! My suggestion is to make a double batch; they never go to waste, as they reheat beautifully.

PESTO-SMASHED POTATOES

DAIRY-FREE/GLUTEN-FREE/KETO/PALEO/VEGAN

SERVES 4-6

1kg baby potatoes

3 tbsp avocado oil, plus extra for drizzling

2 tsp pink salt

1 tsp garlic granules

1 tsp onion granules

1 tsp dried oregano

3–4 heaped tbsp Pesto (page 156), to taste

TIP

Feel free to substitute with chunky chopped sweet potatoes.

1 Preheat the oven to 220°C (200°C fan oven) Gas 7 and line a baking tray with baking paper. Put the potatoes in a bowl and add the oil, salt and flavourings, except the pesto. Coat them well, ensuring that they are well covered.

2 Spread them out on the prepared baking tray, leaving space between each to crisp.

3 Bake for 30 minutes or until crisp on the outside and soft inside.

4 Remove them from the oven and, using the bottom of a metal measuring cup or a glass/porcelain ramekin, press down and squash each potato (I have to admit, this is so incredibly satisfying).

5 Add a drizzle of oil, then randomly dot on the pesto.

6 Return the potatoes to the oven and roast for a further 10 minutes or until crisp. Serve.

Dips, Condiments & Spreads

My husband, Derek, is convinced that he dislikes aubergine, yet every time I make this dip he dives into it and comments on how delicious it is. When roasted aubergine is mixed with tahini and gorgeous Middle Eastern spices, a beautiful harmony happens that will definitely have your family asking for more

BABA GANOUSH

DAIRY-FREE/GLUTEN-FREE/KETO/PALEO/VEGAN

SERVES 4

2 aubergines

2 tbsp avocado oil, plus extra for drizzling

1–2 garlic cloves, to taste, crushed

3 tbsp lemon juice

3 tbsp tahini

4 tbsp extra virgin olive oil or avocado oil

4 tbsp chopped fresh parsley, plus extra to garnish

½ tsp pink salt

½ tsp harissa or za'atar spice blend

½ tsp smoked paprika, plus extra to sprinkle

1 Preheat the oven to 200°C (180°C fan oven) Gas 6. Cut the aubergines in half lengthways, and brush with the oil. Put on a baking tray and bake for 45 minutes or until soft, golden and scoopable, then remove from the oven and leave to cool completely.

2 Once cooled, scrape the flesh away from the skin and put into a bowl. Discard the skin. Mash the flesh with a fork, then add the remaining ingredients and mix well.

3 Serve with an extra drizzle of oil, a sprinkle of fresh parsley and paprika.

When it comes to making a pâté, this recipe really could not get any easier. Not only is mackerel punchy and tasty, but also, being an oily fish, it is loaded with essential omega-3 oils. I love to make a bowl of this and have it on a slice of Olive Oil Keto Bread (page 192) for lunch.

MACKEREL PÂTÉ

DAIRY-FREE/GLUTEN-FREE/KETO/PALEO

SERVES 2

1 large or 2 small shallots, chopped

110g tin mackerel

4 tbsp mayonnaise (with oysters or plain, page 163)

a squeeze of lemon juice, to taste

pink salt and ground black pepper

1 tbsp fresh chopped parsley, to garnish

1 Put all the ingredients in a blender and season with salt and pepper to taste. Blitz to your desired texture. Serve garnished with the parsley.

Although we might follow a dairy-free diet, I still make room in my fridge for kefir cheese, which is a fermented soft-cheese product that is rich in bacteria, lactic acid and natural antibiotics. During the fermentation process the bacteria breaks the lactose down, making it easier to digest. It has a deliciously creamy texture, somewhere between a yogurt and a soft cream cheese, and it can be found either in the yogurt or cheese section of larger supermarkets. If you can't tolerate any form of dairy at all, a nut or coconut cream cheese is a great alternative.

SALMON AND KEFIR DIP

DAIRY-FREE/GLUTEN-FREE/KETO/PALEO

MAKES A SMALL BOWL

150g kefir soft cheese, or a non-dairy cream cheese alternative or thick coconut yogurt

100g smoked salmon

2 tbsp capers

a dash of Tabasco sauce, to taste (I like mine with a good splash)

lemon juice, to taste

1 or 2 sprigs of dill, to taste, chopped

1 Put all the ingredients into a food processor or blender and pulse until smooth. Taste and adjust the flavours according to your preference. Serve.

When I was little, growing up in Zimbabwe, we had an avocado tree in our back garden near our kitchen, which I used to climb and then hang out in the fork of two branches. I didn't really care for the fruit that it produced, but I remember my mum being so excited about the huge avos, and she was always handing them out with glee to friends. Little did I know then how much I would grow to love this fruit, and thankfully I've passed this love on to my girls, who hardly ever go a day without having some form of avocado.

Many memes have been made about how quickly avocados change from ripe to overripe in what seems like a matter of hours. At least if this happens, it's not a waste, because what better way to use your overripe avocados than to turn them into guac?

GUACAMOLE
DAIRY-FREE/GLUTEN-FREE/KETO/PALEO/VEGAN

MAKES 1 MEDIUM-SIZED BOWL

2 ripe–overripe avocados

¼ red onion, finely chopped

1 plum tomato, seeded and chopped

a handful of fresh herbs (coriander or parsley), leaves chopped

juice of 1 lime, or to taste

¼ tsp pink salt

1 tsp white balsamic vinegar or raw apple cider vinegar

1 tsp dried chilli flakes

½ tsp garlic powder

Mixed Seed Crackers (page 253) or a slice of Olive Oil Keto Bread (page 192), to serve

1 Halve the avocados and remove the stones. Scoop out the flesh using a tablespoon and put it into a bowl. Mash the flesh with a fork.

2 Mix in the remaining ingredients. Serve with seeded crackers or on a slice of olive oil bread.

TIP

It's a funny thing how the flavours in guac can be rather personal – feel free to play around with different quantities of these ingredients to make your own preferred flavour and taste.

Salsa is traditionally made with tomatoes and raw onion, but I personally find raw onion to be extremely overpowering, and have always preferred to leave it out. I started to make this onion-free salsa at least 15 years ago, and the recipe has been requested by many friends since that time; one friend, Adam, even asked for a spoon and proceeded to eat it like a gazpacho.

Adding peach is a new thing – I love how it now has the perfect balance of tomato acidity with fruity sweetness.

PEACH AND TOMATO SALSA

DAIRY-FREE/GLUTEN-FREE/KETO/PALEO/VEGAN

MAKES 1 LARGE BOWL

2 ripe yellow peaches, pits removed, chopped

500g cherry tomatoes (in a variety of mixed colours, if possible)

60ml avocado oil

juice of 1–2 limes, to taste

1 red chilli, or to taste, seeded and chopped

1 green chilli, or to taste, seeded and chopped

1 tsp pink or rock salt, or to taste

1 tbsp white balsamic vinegar, or to taste

a generous handful of fresh coriander, leaves chopped

gluten-free corn nachos, to serve

1 Put all the ingredients into a food processor or blender and blitz for a couple of short bursts, scraping down the sides and mixing it up before doing so again.

2 Taste the salsa and decide if it needs more flavour or seasoning, adding more if needed.

3 Transfer to a bowl and leave in the fridge to chill for at least 1 hour if possible before serving; the flavours really enhance with time and just get better the longer they stand. You might need to drain off some of the juices before serving. Serve with gluten-free nachos, or Mixed Seed Crackers (page 253).

One of the wonders of this incredibly versatile vegetable is that it makes a delicious hummus that is easy on the gut. Besides being delicious as it stands, this low-carb hummus also makes a great base for adding other exciting flavours – think roasted red peppers, caramelised onion or sun-dried tomatoes. If you are not that experimental when it comes to cooking, this might be your breakout recipe to have a go at playing around with flavours.

CAULIFLOWER HUMMUS

DAIRY-FREE/GLUTEN-FREE/KETO/PALEO/VEGAN

MAKES 1 MEDIUM BOWL

300g cauliflower, cut into florets

4 tbsp light tahini

3 tbsp lemon juice, or to taste

3 tbsp avocado oil or extra virgin olive oil, plus extra to drizzle

1–2 garlic cloves, to taste, crushed

½ tsp harissa powder or paste (or paprika), plus extra to sprinkle

pink salt and ground black pepper

roasted broccoli or fresh sliced veggies, to serve

1 Steam, boil or microwave the cauliflower until soft. Drain well, then put into a blender or food processor. Add the remaining ingredients and blitz until smooth. Taste and adjust the seasoning if needed.

2 Top with an extra drizzle of oil and a sprinkle of harissa or paprika and serve with roasted broccoli or sliced veggies for dipping.

This traditional sauce is an incredibly versatile condiment to have on hand. It adds a fantastic boost of flavour to so many dishes. I've always loved Worcestershire sauce and remember as a child sipping it neat off a teaspoon. Given that regular store-bought sauces contain sugar and gluten, it is definitely a sauce worth making at home for your family.

WORCESTERSHIRE SAUCE

DAIRY-FREE/GLUTEN-FREE/KETO/PALEO/VEGAN

MAKES 1 SMALL BOTTLE

250ml raw apple cider vinegar

60ml coconut aminos

3 tsp mustard powder

1 tsp garlic granules

½ tsp ground black pepper

2 tbsp blackstrap molasses

¼ tsp ground cinnamon

2 tsp arrowroot powder

1 Put all the ingredients in a saucepan and add 60ml water. Heat over a medium heat until thick, whisking or stirring regularly.

2 Leave to cool then transfer to a recycled sauce bottle or a 300ml jar, and store in the fridge for up to 3 weeks.

Spring is our favourite season, not just because of all the new flowers and growth but because it's wild garlic season. The woods at the bottom of our house become awash with a massive field of wild garlic. I love to pop down first thing in the morning on a dog walk with Jack and grab a basketful to make into pesto. I'll make loads of pesto during this season because the wild garlic lasts only a few weeks, and then we have to wait a whole year until spring for it to return. Nasturtium leaves or nettles also make a fantastic pesto; otherwise trusty, reliable basil from the supermarket is my fail-safe for all-year-round pesto.

The other reason for making my own pesto is that Kyra has a strange allergy to pine nuts. She gets what's called 'pine mouth', which is an intense metallic taste that can last anywhere from two days to two weeks; basically it's like sucking on a bunch of old coins. Anything she eats or drinks during this time makes the metallic taste worse, making life pretty nasty for the duration. For this reason, I don't use pine nuts. I will make the pesto with whatever nuts I have in the pantry, either walnuts, pistachio nuts or cashew nuts.

PESTO

DAIRY-FREE/GLUTEN-FREE/KETO/PALEO/VEGAN

MAKES A 500ML JAR

100g basil leaves or any leaves of choice

100g raw walnuts, or pistachio nuts or cashew nuts

2 tsp garlic powder or 2 garlic cloves, crushed

60ml lemon juice

3 tbsp nutritional yeast flakes

1 tsp pink salt

185ml extra virgin olive or avocado oil

1 Put the basil in a food processor or blender and add the, nuts, garlic, lemon juice, nutritional yeast flakes and salt. Blend while slowly drizzling in the oil. Store in a jar in the fridge for up to 3 weeks.

A Healthier Family for Life | Dips, Condiments & Spreads

Use store-bought berry, lemon or ginger kombucha to add a lovely sweet flavour to the pickling solution. The onions work well with so many dishes, from salads to pesto-roasted salmon, or on Friday-night pizzas. Save a few spoonfuls of the kombucha liquid to drizzle over a salad as a dressing; not only is it super-delicious but it is also incredibly gut friendly. It's one of the most popular recipes on my website – it takes minutes to prepare and is another staple in our fridge.

KOMBUCHA PICKLED RED ONION

DAIRY-FREE/GLUTEN-FREE/KETO/PALEO/VEGAN

MAKES 1 LARGE JAR

4 red onions, thinly sliced

1–2 tbsp raw honey to taste, or sweetener (optional)

a few sprigs of fresh rosemary

2–3 garlic cloves, to taste, sliced

2.5cm fresh ginger, or to taste, peeled and grated

250ml raw apple cider vinegar

400ml lemon, berry or ginger kombucha

FOR THE PICKLING SPICES

1 tsp black peppercorns

1 tsp mustard seeds

1 tsp dried chilli flakes (optional)

1 tsp ground turmeric

12 bay leaves

1 tsp whole cloves (optional)

1 star anise (optional)

1 tsp pink or rock salt

1 Put the onions in a saucepan of boiling water for 1 minute to blanch them, then remove them immediately and leave to cool.

2 Put the onions in a 1 litre sealable jar, and add the honey, rosemary, garlic and ginger, and the pickling spices, including the salt.

3 Pour in the vinegar and kombucha, and press down on the onions until they are fully immersed in the liquid. Seal and store in the fridge for up to 1 month.

TIP

If you have access to wild garlic flower buds, nasturtium or chive flowers, they make a beautiful and super-tasty addition to the pickling solution.

"The oysters that Seymour Oysters cultivate are grown a mile offshore in the Bay of Grouville. This is on the Eastern coast of Jersey, just South of the old small fishing village, Gorey, overlooked for the last 800 years by the grand Mont Orgueil Castle. The oysters are mainly grown from seed and reared in mesh bags laid on trestle tables, which sit freely on the seabed. Nothing is added, they grow from the beauty of nature to create their unique, slightly salty flavour loved all over the world.

Seymour Oysters' beds are amongst the largest oyster beds in Europe and enjoy a picturesque setting, the wildlife is already considerable and the presence of the oyster tables enhances the biodiversity of the flora and fauna in the area.

Shannon and John Le Seelleur, Jersey Oyster Farmers

My friends Shannon and John Le Seelleur own and run one of the largest oyster farms in Europe: Seymour Oysters. Shannon runs champagne-and-oyster walking tours, and it's always great to listen to her talk about the history of Jersey, the incredible tidal range, and the health benefits of oysters – and then my favourite part is to watch and marvel as she shucks oysters with ease. I just had to include a recipe with oysters in my book to honour these amazing farmers.

Oysters add an incredible flavour and lightness to mayonnaise without being overbearing. They give it almost an indescribable saltiness. It's also an ideal way to get essential nutrients and minerals into little (or big) fussy eaters without them even knowing. If oysters really aren't your thing, or they don't fit into your budget, absolutely feel free to leave them out – they don't change the recipe; they simply add to it.

An immersion or high-speed blender is needed for making this recipe.

OYSTER MAYONNAISE

DAIRY-FREE/GLUTEN-FREE/KETO/PALEO

MAKES 1 SMALL JAR

2 freshly shucked oysters

1 egg and 1 egg yolk

1 tbsp raw apple cider vinegar

1 tsp mustard powder

2 tsp Tabasco sauce or any other chilli sauce (optional)

½ tsp pink salt

250ml light olive oil (not extra virgin – the flavour is too strong)

TIP

Use this recipe without the oysters, if you prefer, as a basic mayonnaise for other recipes in the book.

1 You can make the recipe without using oysters to give you a plain mayonnaise, if you prefer. Using your fingers, remove the oysters from their shells and wash them, ensuring that there are no shell fragments on them at all.

2 Put all the ingredients, except the oil, into a blender jug and blend well. Very slowly pour in the oil in a fine stream while blending. Once the emulsion starts to happen (it changes from yellow to white and thickens immediately), if you are using an immersion blender, very gently move it from side to side to allow the oil to move into the spaces. Slowly start to bring your blender up towards the top of the emulsion allowing all the oil to blend in.

3 Bottle in a recycled jam jar and store in the fridge. If using oysters, eat the mayonnaise within a few days of making, otherwise the mayonnaise can keep for about 2 weeks in the fridge.

As a child I would smother my food with tomato sauce, so I don't take offence against anyone who wants to add a little flavour boost to their food. Homemade ketchup is not only easy to make and a fun afternoon activity for little hands, but it's also utterly delicious, and the best part is that you are totally in control about what goes into it.

This recipe is incredibly versatile and is not just a ketchup: a bottle in the fridge can be used for a last-minute pizza sauce, or you can add it to stews or bolognese dishes, or even over noodles or zoodles (courgette noodles).

TOMATO SAUCE

DAIRY-FREE/GLUTEN-FREE/KETO/PALEO/VEGAN

MAKES TWO 500ML JARS

100g (about 5) fresh, soft Medjool dates, or dried unsweetened dates soaked in warm water until soft, pitted and chopped

1 tbsp avocado oil

1 large onion, finely chopped

700g tomato passata

125ml raw apple cider vinegar

70g tomato purée

1 tbsp garlic granules or 3 garlic cloves, crushed

1 tbsp pink salt

1 tsp ground cinnamon

1 tsp paprika

1 Soak the dates in a bowl with 125ml hot water for 10 minutes to soften them. Heat the oil in a saucepan over a medium-high heat and cook the onion for 5 minutes or until soft.

2 Mash the dates with a fork, add the dates and water to the onions, then remove the pan from the heat.

3 Add the remaining ingredients and, using an immersion blender, blend until smooth.

4 Cover the saucepan with a lid and cook over a medium heat for 10–15 minutes until bubbling and thickened. Leave to cool then transfer to recycled sauce jars and store in the fridge for up to 3 weeks.

Childhood memories of eating lemon curd with my precious grandma stir up a wave of happy emotions in me. I do love having a jar in the fridge to dollop onto pancakes or a slice of keto toast (see page 192).

Use only the best-quality free-range chicken or duck eggs that you can find, because eggs of this quality will have a naturally gorgeous bright-orange yolk, which transfers through to the end result: a glorious bright-yellow curd.

LEMON CURD

DAIRY-FREE/GLUTEN-FREE/KETO/PALEO

MAKES ONE 250ML JAR

80ml coconut oil

3–4 tbsp raw honey, or maple syrup or sweetener, to taste

125ml lemon juice

3 free-range eggs or 2 free-range duck eggs

TIPS

Strain the curd through a sieve if any eggy bits have formed. This will happen if the pan is too hot or the mixture is overcooked.

Add 1 tsp powdered grass-fed gelatin and use it as an icing for cupcakes.

1 Melt the coconut oil and honey in a heavy-based saucepan over a very low heat.

2 Add the lemon juice and mix well.

3 Whisk the eggs and add to the oil mixture, then turn up the heat to medium.

4 Continue whisking or stirring until the mixture starts to thicken. It will thicken to the point when stirring it will leave tracks.

5 Remove from the heat and leave to cool, stirring occasionally. Bottle it in a groovy recycled honey jar and pop it into the fridge. Use within 2 weeks.

Making jam could honestly not be easier. Okay, this is not a very traditional way of making it, but then again I guess we eat in an untraditional way in our house. Jam is normally a scientific balance between fruit, sugar and temperature, which gives it a gooey, sticky consistency. In this recipe I leave the natural sugar in the fruit to provide sweetness and rely on lemon peel and gelatin or agar-agar to achieve the jam consistency. Roasting it in the oven makes for a deliciously tasty version that is just so easy and fuss-free.

I get my jamming strawberries from my local pick-your-own farm, where they often have trays at the back of the store during strawberry season. These are 'seconds', or strawberries that are badly bruised or a day or two away from turning. They are not always the prettiest to look at, but they are certainly the best to use for jam, as they are at their ripest and richest in flavour. I suggest popping into your local greengrocer or supermarket and enquiring if they have any trays of older strawberries; I'm sure they would be very happy for you to take them off their hands at a discount.

OVEN-ROASTED STRAWBERRY JAM

DAIRY-FREE/GLUTEN-FREE/KETO/PALEO/VEGAN

MAKES ABOUT THREE 500ML JARS

2kg jamming or old strawberries, hulled

3 tbsp raw honey or maple syrup

3 tbsp vanilla extract

1 large lemon, roughly chopped into quarters and pips removed

1 tbsp powdered grass-fed gelatin or 1 tsp agar-agar

1 Preheat the oven to 200°C (180°C fan oven) Gas 6. Put the strawberries in a large roasting tin and add the honey, vanilla and lemon, then give it a good mixing up. Roast for 1½ hours. Put 3 tbsp water in a small bowl and add the gelatin. Mix well until dissolved. Remove the strawberries from the oven and stir the gelatin mixture through, then leave to cool. Transfer the jam to sterilised recycled jars, cover and leave to cool. Use within 2 weeks.

The ultimate compliment for me is when someone really loves something that I make. Andy, Gemma's boyfriend, has been vegan for many years and always talks about this caramel sauce. In fact, when he visits, he sits down with the saucepan and spoon and eats it as a pudding on its own.

This is what Andy wrote about my sauce: 'When I first tried this caramel it instantly reminded me of the decadent desserts that I used to love before I went vegan. It's such a great feeling to find something that satisfies your sweet tooth in just the right way – it's perfectly rich and creamy and doesn't take too long to prepare. This caramel may even be one of the best homemade vegan treats I've ever tried!'

Wow! Thanks, Andy!

SALTED CARAMEL SAUCE

DAIRY-FREE/GLUTEN-FREE/PALEO/VEGAN

MAKES 1 SMALL JAR

400ml tinned coconut milk

50g coconut sugar

1 tbsp coconut oil

1 tbsp vanilla extract

1ml ground pink salt

TIP.

For a richer, thicker caramel, transfer the cooked caramel to a microwavable glass container and microwave at full power for 1 minute. I know it might seem strange, but it really takes this sauce to the next level!

1 Put the coconut milk in a small saucepan and add the sugar and oil. Bring to the boil over a medium-high heat. Allow it to boil for 3–4 minutes until it starts to get a really good bubble going, stirring continuously, then reduce the heat to a gentle simmer, stirring occasionally, for 50–60 minutes until it reduces to about half and thickens.

2 Turn off the heat, stir in the vanilla and salt, then leave it to cool for 1 hour. Cover and chill in the fridge overnight where it will continue to thicken.

This quick dairy-free chocolate sauce ticks all the boxes: it's smooth, velvety and just downright divine. Drizzle it warm over ice cream, crêpes or pancakes; dunk strawberries in it; or my girls love to have it cooled on their bread or toast as a chocolate spread. Any leftovers can be stored in the fridge for up to a week – be aware that it will go solid, so it will need to be put in the microwave for 30 seconds before serving – although I don't think it will last long enough to require refrigeration.

CHOCOLATE SAUCE

DAIRY-FREE/GLUTEN-FREE/KETO/PALEO/VEGAN

SERVES 2

2 tbsp coconut oil

2 tbsp raw honey, or maple syrup or powdered sweetener

3 tbsp raw cacao powder

3 tbsp canned coconut cream

1 Melt the coconut oil and honey in a saucepan over a low heat or in a microwave.

2 Whisk the cacao through the mixture, then allow it to cool slightly (it might be slightly grainy, but don't worry).

3 Whisk through the coconut cream and the grain should disappear and magically transform to a smooth and velvety texture. Serve warm or cooled.

Perfectly whipped coconut cream is a fantastic dairy-free alternative. Let's be honest, so many dishes are made better with a big dollop of whipped cream. A good quality, full-fat can of coconut milk and a night in the fridge is what's needed to get the cream light and fluffy with soft peaks. Be careful of adding too much liquid sweetener (honey or maple syrup) – you don't want anything that could weigh it down. Also, I find it best to select a can of coconut in store that feels solid when shaken. Start preparations the night before.

WHIPPED COCONUT CREAM

DAIRY-FREE/GLUTEN-FREE/KETO/PALEO/VEGAN

MAKES 1 SMALL BOWL

400ml can full-fat coconut milk

1 tsp vanilla powder or extract

1–2 tsp coconut sugar, or raw honey or sweetener, to taste

TIP

If you have a metal mixing bowl, pop it in the freezer to chill before whipping – it will make the cream easier to whip. Not all coconut milk brands are the same; the success of this cream depends on the brand that you purchase.

1 It's absolutely essential that the can of coconut milk stands upright overnight in the fridge – sadly the freezer won't work. You know it's set hard when you shake it and there is no movement – that's when you can take it out and whip it.

2 Using a spoon, carefully scrape all the cream from the top of the can, leaving the water behind (you can save it for your Green Juice on page 60).

3 Add the remaining ingredients and whip until light and peaks form. Use immediately or chill in the fridge; it will harden and set in the fridge the longer it's chilled. Use within 2 weeks.

Bakes, Puddings & Snacks

This is without a doubt a showstopper cake. I just love the chocolatey flavour combination of coffee and pear, accentuated by the malty flavour from the blackstrap molasses. Blackstrap molasses is a dark viscous liquid that is the by-product of the sugar cane refining process. Before you start to panic at the 'S' word, don't worry – it's the good stuff, and it has the lowest sugar content of any sugar-cane product. Actually, it has numerous health benefits, because it contains a range of vital vitamins and minerals.

Serve this cake cold, or warmed with non-dairy ice cream or a drizzle of White Chocolate Sauce from page 216.

PEAR AND COFFEE LOAF

DAIRY-FREE/GLUTEN-FREE/PALEO

MAKES 12 PORTIONS

2–3 ripe Conference pears (depending on size)

150g almond flour or ground almonds

70g cassava flour

50g raw cacao powder

1 tsp bicarbonate of soda

a pinch of pink salt

40g coconut sugar or dry sweetener

3 free-range eggs

2 tbsp blackstrap molasses

¼ cup avocado oil or melted coconut oil, plus extra for greasing

1 tsp raw apple cider vinegar

250ml cold black coffee

1 Preheat the oven to 180°C (160°C fan oven) Gas 4. Grease and line a 900g loaf tin with baking paper. Test that the pears fit the tin by standing them upright in a row to confirm that they fit comfortably with space around them – you don't want them to be touching each other

2 Peel the pears and, leaving them whole, cut off the bases to make them flat so that they can stand upright without wobbling over.

3 In a bowl sift together the almond flour, cassava flour, cacao powder, bicarbonate of soda, salt and coconut sugar.

4 In a separate bowl, whisk together the eggs, molasses, avocado oil and vinegar.

5 Add the wet ingredients to the dry ingredients, then add the coffee. Stir the batter well.

6 Pour the batter into the prepared tin and insert the pears in a standing position in a row, pushing them all the way down to the base. Bake for 40 minutes or until a cocktail stick inserted into the cake part comes out clean and the cake feels springy to the touch. Gently remove from the tin and serve warm or cold.

You certainly don't need a celebration to bake this cake, but following an alternative diet definitely complicates things when it comes time to blow out your candles. Grain-free baking uses calorie-dense ingredients, so smaller slices are all that's needed.

This cake is smaller in size: I use three 15cm-wide cake tins, which is not uncommon for artisan-style cakes and it looks beautiful. Feel free to use whatever tins you have available, anything from a single bundt tin, two sandwich tins or three smaller artisan-style tins work well.

Heads up: make the icing a day before to allow it to set; it will save you a lot of stress making it in advance.

CELEBRATION CHOCOLATE CAKE

DAIRY-FREE/GLUTEN-FREE/PALEO

MAKES 12 PORTIONS

4 free-range eggs, separated

125ml nut milk

250ml black coffee, cooled

125ml avocado oil or extra virgin olive oil

100g coconut sugar

50g cocoa

200g almond flour

100g cassava flour

2 tsp gluten-free baking powder

½ tsp pink salt

(continued over page)

1 Make the icing a day ahead to allow it to set. Heat the coconut milk and vanilla extract in a saucepan over a medium heat until it starts to steam, then whisk through the gelatin, add the chocolate chips and salt, then leave it to stand for a few minutes. Stir well, making sure that all the chocolate is melted, then stir in chopped hazelnuts, if using. Transfer to a glass bowl and allow it to cool uncovered in the fridge until firm.

2 Preheat the oven to 170°C (150°C fan oven) Gas 3 and prepare three 15cm cake tins (or two sandwich tins, or a single bundt tin) by either giving them a good wipe down with coconut oil or lining with baking paper. In a stand mixer or in a bowl using an electric or hand whisk, whisk the egg whites until stiff peaks form, then transfer to a smaller bowl and set aside.

3 Put the egg yolks in the bowl and add the milk, coffee and oil, then beat well. Sift the sugar, cocoa, almond flour, cassava flour, baking powder and salt into a separate bowl.

4 Spoon the dry ingredients into the wet ingredients, one heaped spoon at a time, and mix using the mixer on slow or using a wooden spoon.

5 Stop the mixer and fold through the egg whites (stirring in a figure-of-eight movement).

(continued over page)

6 Transfer the batter to your prepared baking tins and follow the schedule below for baking times (it changes depending on how many tins you use):

3 tins: 30 minutes

2 tins: 30–35 minutes

bundt tin: 35–40 minutes

7 The cake is cooked when a cocktail stick inserted into the centre comes out clean. It will also feel firm when pressed. Allow for extra time if not firm. Leave on a wire rack to cool entirely before removing the cake from the tin. When the cake is completely cold, cover with the icing and let the celebrations begin!

FOR THE ICING

480g coconut cream

2 tsp vanilla extract

1 tsp powdered grass-fed gelatin or ½ tsp agar-agar

250g dairy-free dark chocolate chips

a pinch of pink salt

100g chopped hazelnuts (optional)

TIP

Top with extra hazelnuts, fresh berries and edible flowers to add that extra wow factor.

For many years we went without mince pies at Christmas. My family nagged me to come up with a recipe for them to be able to enjoy this Christmastime treat, but of course it didn't just have to be gluten-free but also dairy- and sugar-free to keep everyone happy. The fruit mince here is flavoured with tart green apples, either Granny Smiths or Bramley apples, orange zest and a splash of brandy to infuse it with the Christmas spirit.

You can choose which pastry you prefer to use: vegan or non-vegan. Both work well with this recipe. If the thought of making small tarts terrifies you, or you are short of time, simply make one big tart in a 23cm tin and bake for the same amount of time, then slice it up. It important to start preparations the day before, giving all the gorgeous flavours time to activate.

FRUIT MINCE PIES

DAIRY-FREE/GLUTEN-FREE/PALEO/VEGAN

MAKES 12–15 PIES

1 x quantity vegan or non-vegan pastry (page 199)

tapioca flour, to sprinkle (optional)

FOR THE APPLE FRUIT MINCE

2 tbsp coconut oil

3 small Granny Smith apples or 2 large Bramley apples, unpeeled and grated

zest and juice of 1 large orange

300g sultanas or raisins

1–2 tbsp raw honey, to taste

2 tsp ground cinnamon

1 tsp ground ginger

(continued over page)

1 The fruit mince can be made in advance and kept in the fridge (depending on the size of the apples there is usually enough for two batches). Heat a saucepan over a medium-high heat and melt the coconut oil and fry the apples for 1 minute to soften.

2 Add the orange zest and juice and mix well. Reduce the heat to low. Add 60ml water and the remaining ingredients, except the brandy.

3 Mix everything together, then cover and leave to simmer gently for 20–30 minutes, stirring once or twice, but not too often as the raisins can turn into a paste if overworked. It is ready when the raisins are plump and soft.

4 Stir through the brandy, if using. Leave to cool, then store in a jar in the fridge.

5 Preheat the oven to 170°C (150°C fan oven) Gas 3. Grease a 12-cup muffin tray.

6 Make the vegan pastry as explained in steps 2 and 3 or the non-vegan pastry as in steps 2–4 of the pastry recipes on page 199.

(continued over page)

1 tsp freshly grated
nutmeg

¼ tsp ground cloves

2–4 tbsp brandy, to taste
(optional)

TIP

One jar of fruit mince is
enough for two batches of
mince pies. If there is not
enough for a second
batch, simply steam and
mash more apples to
boost the volume.

7 Scrape the dough contents out of the food processor and knead the dough slightly on a silicon mat or a sheet of baking paper.

8 Shape it into a large ball, then flatten it as much as possible. Add a second sheet of baking paper and, using a rolling pin, roll from the centre out until it is about 5mm thick.

9 Remove the top sheet, then use a 9cm pastry cutter to cut 12 discs. Use a smaller pastry cutter to cut circles or decorative toppings (such as stars) from the remaining pastry.

10 Line each muffin cup with the larger pastry disc. Fill with fruit mince, then add the pastry top (you don't have to cover the top, you can use the pastry to make extra pies as tarts with no lid). Bake for 30 minutes. Top with a dusting of tapioca flour, if you like, for extra Christmas spirit, and enjoy.

Regardless of whether you are serving this for Easter (although not traditional it has recently become popular as an Easter cake) or any other occasion, this cake is honestly the best thing ever to bring out and share with friends. I have worked really hard on creating a cake that is not dry and crumbly, but rather incredibly moist and really easy to whip up for all the family or for friends.

CARROT CAKE

DAIRY-FREE/GLUTEN-FREE/PALEO

MAKES 12 PORTIONS

100g fresh Medjool dates, or dried unsweetened dates soaked in warm water until soft, pitted and chopped

300g ground almonds

40g coconut sugar, or a few extra dates for sweetness

2 tsp ground cinnamon

1 tsp ground allspice

2 tsp bicarbonate of soda

4 free-range eggs, at room temperature

125ml coconut oil, melted or runny, plus extra for greasing

2 tsp raw apple cider vinegar

1 tbsp vanilla extract

100g walnuts or pecan nuts, chopped

400g carrots, grated

edible flowers, chopped carrot tops or desiccated coconut, to decorate (optional)

1 Preheat the oven to 170°C (150°C fan oven) Gas 3. Grease a 20cm loose-based cake tin and line the base with baking paper. Put the dates in a food processor or blender and add the ground almonds, coconut sugar, spices and bicarbonate of soda. Blend together just for a second or two or for a few pulse bursts so that everything is mixed and chopped, then transfer to a mixing bowl.

2 Put the eggs into the food processor or blender, and add the coconut oil, vinegar and vanilla extract. Blitz for a few seconds until everything is mixed together.

3 Stir the chopped nuts and grated carrots into the egg mixture, then pour the mixture into the bowl with the dry ingredients and gently mix everything together to form a batter.

4 Transfer the batter to the prepared baking tin. Bake for 1 hour or until a cocktail stick inserted into the centre comes out clean. Remove from the oven and leave to cool in the tin on a wire rack (don't try and remove it too soon or it might fall apart).

5 In a bowl, mix together the icing ingredients. Put in the fridge until the cake is totally cooled and ready to be assembled.

6 Once cooled, slice the cake in half horizontally (it might seem slightly undercooked, but this is the way it should be for a moist carrot cake).

7 Use half the icing in the middle and roughly spread it, allowing it to spill over the edge.

8 Put the other half of the cake on top and cover with the remaining icing. Decorate with edible flowers, chopped carrot tops or simply sprinkle desiccated coconut, if you like.

FOR THE ICING

340g nut or coconut cream cheese (at room temperature) or refrigerated full-fat coconut milk (see Whipped Coconut Cream page 173)

2 tbsp lemon juice

zest of 1 lemon, or to taste

2 tbsp raw honey or maple syrup

1 tsp vanilla extract

TIP

The cake can also be baked in a baking tray and served as a traybake.

This cake recipe is versatile and can be used for cupcakes, as a base for trifle or almost any recipe that calls for a simple vanilla cake. The jam is easy to prepare and any leftovers can be kept in the fridge for a midnight snack with cashew butter. The whipped coconut cream is just heavenly and delicious – enough said, just give it a go!

VANILLA SPONGE WITH BERRY JAM

DAIRY-FREE/GLUTEN-FREE/PALEO

MAKES 12 PORTIONS

4 free-range eggs, separated

100g coconut sugar

125ml olive oil or melted coconut oil, plus extra for greasing

250ml nut milk

2 tsp vanilla extract

2 tsp raw apple cider vinegar

100g cassava flour

200g almond flour

2 tsp bicarbonate of soda

FOR THE STRAWBERRY JAM

1 tsp vanilla extract or rose extract

2 tbsp raw honey

2 tsp powdered grass-fed gelatin or ½ tsp agar-agar

500g strawberries, hulled and quartered

1 lemon, halved

FOR THE CREAM TOPPING

400ml Whipped Coconut Cream (page 173)

1 To make the strawberry jam, put the vanilla, honey and gelatin in a saucepan and add 60ml water. Give everything a good stir to incorporate the gelatin so that it does not become lumpy.

2 Add the strawberries and lemon halves and put the pan over a medium heat. Leave the jam to bubble away, stirring regularly until the juices are reduced and turn to a jam consistency. If needed, turn up the heat to achieve a good bubble. It will go through stages where it looks really pale and the strawberries almost turn white; just keep going, as it will eventually caramelise and turn a beautiful red colour. This will take about 20 minutes.

3 Remove the lemon and discard. Transfer the jam to a sterilised glass jar or bowl and leave it to cool, then chill it in the fridge.

4 Preheat the oven to 170°C (150°C fan oven) Gas 3. Grease two sandwich tins and line the bases with baking paper. Whisk the separated egg whites in a large bowl until stiff and firm, using an electric or hand whisk, then set aside.

5 Put the egg yolks in another bowl and add the sugar, oil, milk, 125ml water, the vanilla and apple cider vinegar. Whisk together.

6 Sift in the flours and bicarbonate of soda, then stir well.

7 Spoon in the whisked egg white and mix gently in a figure-of-eight movement.

8 Divide the batter between the prepared sandwich tins and bake for 30 minutes or until golden brown and a cocktail stick inserted into the centre comes out clean. Remove the cakes from the tin and leave on a wire rack to cool.

9 Spread the strawberry jam over the top of one cake and then spread over the whipped coconut cream. Put the second cake on top.

Over the years, I have made numerous cakes from this recipe, and they work beautifully every time. Super simple and easy, I guarantee that your family will go bonkers for it!

This doesn't need to be made up weeks before Christmas, although I do suggest giving the raisins a good soak in brandy for a day or two before baking.

GRAIN-FREE CHRISTMAS CAKE

DAIRY-FREE/GLUTEN-FREE/PALEO

MAKES 12–15 PORTIONS

300g raisins or sultanas

250ml brandy or orange juice

4 free-range eggs

125ml extra virgin olive oil, plus extra for greasing

1 tbsp vanilla extract

1 tsp almond extract

300g almond flour

50g coconut sugar

1 tbsp gluten-free baking powder

1 tbsp ground cinnamon

1½ tsp ground ginger

1 tsp freshly grated nutmeg

½ tsp ground cloves

zest of two oranges

280g carrots, grated

100g pecan nuts, chopped

100g cranberries

tapioca or arrowroot powder, a ribbon, fresh berries, edible flowers or rosemary sprigs, to decorate

1 Put the raisins in a bowl and add the brandy. Soak overnight or a day or two before baking. Preheat the oven to 170°C (150°C fan oven) Gas 3. Grease a bundt or 23cm springform cake tin really well, making sure to get into all the little grooves and dents.

2 In a large bowl, beat together the eggs, oil, vanilla and almond extract.

3 Put the almond flour in a separate bowl and add the coconut sugar, baking powder, cinnamon, ginger, nutmeg and cloves. Stir well.

4 Add the dry ingredients to the wet ingredients and mix well.

5 Stir in the orange zest, grated carrots, and the raisins with the soaking liquid.

6 Stir through the pecan nuts and cranberries, then spoon the batter into the prepared cake tin.

7 Bake for 1 hour – but do keep checking it after 45 minutes. (Oven temps vary, so you don't want to burn it. If it starts to look very dark on top yet still not cooked through, put a sheet of baking paper loosely over the top.)

8 Press firmly around all parts of the top of the cake to confirm that it is cooked through; the density should be even throughout the cake (the sides should feel the same as the centre). If it has more give in the centre, bake it for longer.

9 Leave to cool completely before removing it from the tin.

10 To decorate, sprinkle over a dusting of tapioca or arrowroot powder, wrap a festive ribbon around, then add fresh berries, edible flowers or rosemary sprigs.

My family are besotted with cheesecake, Gemma especially. I think giving up her favourite treat was the hardest part of turning vegan. As I've mentioned many times in this book, regardless of your choice of diet or intolerances, you should never have to go without any of your favourite treats, cheesecake included. As simple as this is to make, however, it is a labour of love in that it needs plenty of time and forward planning to soak the cashew nuts – but, trust me, it's worth taking the time because this cheesecake is truly delicious. It will end up being the star of the show! Start preparations the night before.

GEMMA'S BLUEBERRY AND LEMON CHEESECAKE

DAIRY-FREE/GLUTEN-FREE/PALEO/VEGAN

MAKES 12 PORTIONS

For the lemon filling:

400g cashew nuts

zest and juice of 1 lemon, or to taste

120ml coconut kefir, or coconut cream or coconut yogurt

80ml coconut oil, melted

½ tsp agar-agar or 1 tsp powdered grass-fed gelatin

2 tbsp raw honey, maple syrup or sweetener (optional)

1 Soak the cashew nuts for the filling in water overnight, so that they become plump and soft.

2 To make the crust, mix all the ingredients together in a blender or food processor until they form a crumb-like texture, then press them firmly into the base of an 18cm springform cake tin or glass dish using the base of a ramekin or measuring cup to ensure that it is even and flat.

3 To make the filling, drain and discard the cashew water, then put the cashew nuts in a blender or food processor and add the lemon zest and juice and the kefir. Blend to combine.

4 Warm the coconut oil and stir in the agar-agar and mix well until dissolved, then add to the cashew mixture.

5 Blend for a few minutes until as smooth as possible, then taste and add more lemon or sweetener, if needed. Spoon this filling over the crust, then transfer to a freezer for at least 4 hours or until firm.

6 To make the blueberry topping, heat all the topping ingredients together in a saucepan over a medium heat for 10 minutes, occasionally giving it a gentle stir (a jiggle of the pan is actually better) so as not to burst the blueberries.

7 Remove the cheesecake from the freezer and top with the blueberry topping, then put it in the fridge for 1 hour or until the blueberry topping has set to a firm jelly. Then it's ready to serve.

FOR THE CRUST

100g pecan nuts, chopped

50g ground almonds or almond flour

100g (about 5) fresh Medjool dates, or dried unsweetened dates soaked in warm water until soft, pitted and chopped

2 tbsp coconut oil

1 tsp vanilla extract

¼ tsp pink salt

FOR THE BLUEBERRY TOPPING

300g blueberries or berries of your choice

60ml lemon juice (about 1 whole lemon)

1 tbsp coconut oil

1 tbsp raw honey, or maple syrup or sweetener

½ tsp agar-agar or 1 tsp powdered grass-fed gelatin

I've learned that bread is absolutely an essential, even on a healthy-eating plan. We have become so hardwired to have a slice of bread with soup or even a smear of butter and jam as a snack. Now, I'm not saying to rush out and buy a loaf of processed white bread, but rather if you are going to indulge in a slice, make it a healthy nutritious slice that can add to your daily nutritional intake.

OLIVE OIL KETO BREAD

DAIRY-FREE/GLUTEN-FREE/KETO/PALEO/VEGAN

MAKES ONE LOAF

125ml olive oil or avocado oil

1 tsp raw honey

2 tsp fast action/easy-bake dried yeast

200g almond flour

1 tbsp coconut flour

1 tsp pink salt

1 tsp gluten-free baking powder

4 free-range eggs at room temperature

sesame seeds, to sprinkle (optional)

TIP

Make it a deliciously crunchy bread by adding 125g of ground seeds, nuts or shelled hemp hearts.

1 Preheat the oven to 170°C (150°C fan oven) Gas 3, and grease and line a 450g loaf tin with baking paper. In a saucepan, heat the olive oil and honey to bath-water temperature – you should be able to dip in your finger without burning it. Sprinkle in the yeast, give it a little jiggle and set aside.

2 Put the almond flour in a mixing bowl, and add the coconut flour, salt and baking powder. Give it a good stir to mix well.

3 In a bowl, whisk the eggs at high speed for about 2 minutes until frothy. Slowly drizzle the oil mixture into the eggs while continuing to whisk.

4 Add the dry ingredients to the egg mixture a few heaped tablespoonfuls at a time, whisking between additions.

5 Transfer the batter into the prepared baking tin, sprinkle some sesame seeds on top, if you like, and bake for 45 minutes or until golden brown. Cool on a wire rack.

Whenever I make this bread my family goes crazy over it, and it makes the ideal accompaniment for a salad and frittata; try it with chicken livers or even just on its own. There is something so decadent and lush about adding caramelised onions – they are worth taking the time to make.

CARAMELISED ONION FOCACCIA

DAIRY-FREE/GLUTEN-FREE/KETO/PALEO

MAKES 1 FOCACCIA

60ml plus 2 tbsp avocado oil

2 onions, sliced

300g almond flour

2 tbsp psyllium husk

4 tbsp nutritional yeast flakes

1 tsp garlic powder

1 tsp pink salt

1 tsp gluten-free baking powder

3 free-range eggs

250ml coconut yogurt

1 Heat the 2 tbsp oil in a frying pan over a medium-low heat and cook the onions for 30 minutes or until caramelised and sticky (covering the pan while cooking really helps).

2 Preheat the oven to 180°C (160°C fan oven) Gas 4 and grease and line a 20 x 25cm baking tray (I use a silicon baking tray and it works beautifully). In a large mixing bowl, mix together the almond flour, psyllium husk, nutritional yeast flakes, garlic powder, salt and baking powder.

3 In another bowl, whisk together the eggs, 60ml oil and the yogurt. Pour the egg mixture into the dry ingredients and mix well together. Transfer to the prepared baking tray. Top with the caramelised onions.

4 Bake for 30 minutes or until the top of the bread is golden brown and the onions are turning crispy. Turn off the oven and leave the focaccia in the oven to cool down slowly.

If you have never made a loaf of bread before, this is the bread recipe for you. All you do is throw all the ingredients into a bowl, mix and bake. No fancy machines are needed, just strong arms. The raisins add a delicious flavour to the bread, but if you are following a keto diet you can easily leave them out to reduce the carbohydrates. It is incredibly nutrient dense, so only thin slices are needed for deliciously healthy sarnies. Freeze the loaf in pre-cut slices and defrost them when needed.

NORDIC FRUIT AND NUT LOAF

DAIRY-FREE/GLUTEN-FREE/KETO/PALEO

MAKES 1 LOAF

5 free-range eggs

200g mixed nuts (I prefer to use macadamia and walnut), roughly chopped

100g milled flaxseed

100g pumpkin seeds

100g sunflower seeds

50g sesame seeds

100g raisins (optional)

50g tahini

80ml extra virgin olive oil

1 tsp bicarbonate of soda

1 tsp raw apple cider vinegar

1 Preheat the oven to 160°C (140°C fan oven) Gas 3. Line a 900g loaf tin with baking paper – the bread leaves an oily residue so this step is highly recommended for absorption.

2 Put all the ingredients in a large mixing bowl. Using a spatula, mix everything together really well. Transfer the batter to the prepared loaf tin and bake for 1 hour. Remove the loaf and leave on a wire rack to cool.

I never intended to add this as a standalone recipe, but as I started to write I realised that it is a pretty crucial base for many of my recipes. I'm not a trained chef in any way, and like most mums I have little experience working with pastry, so I really wanted to create a recipe that is easy and fuss-free for those of us who are not comfortable around rolling pins.

I find working with a silicon mat much easier, as the dough can simply be rolled up in one direction and then unrolled over the tart tin. If you don't have a silicon mat, a sheet of baking paper works well. With this type of pastry, adding a second sheet of paper over the top before rolling stops the dough from sticking to the rolling pin.

I've included two separate pastries for either vegan or non-vegan; both are easy to work with and have so many uses over and above tart bases. Use them for galettes and sugar biscuits, or omit the sugar to make crispy thin pizza bases or crusts for pies.

PASTRY

DAIRY-FREE/GLUTEN-FREE/KETO/PALEO/VEGAN

MAKES ENOUGH TO
LINE A 23CM TART
TIN/12 MINCE PIES

FOR THE NON-VEGAN
PASTRY

100g cassava flour, plus extra for dusting

200g almond flour

2 tbsp coconut sugar or sweetener

1 tbsp powdered grass-fed gelatin

1 tsp gluten-free baking powder

1 egg

4 tbsp olive oil, or avocado or coconut oil

1 tbsp vanilla extract

(continued over page)

1 To make the non-vegan pastry, preheat the oven to 170°C (150°C fan oven) Gas 3. Grease a 23cm loose-based tart tin.

2 Put all the dry ingredients into a food processor and pulse for 1 second to mix. Add the egg.

3 Put the oil in a bowl and add 125ml hot water and the vanilla extract. Mix together, then pour into the dry ingredients. Blitz the dough until it forms a paste-like batter.

4 Scrape the contents out of the processor with a spatula. It might seem a little wet and sticky, but kneading the dough slightly on a cassava-dusted silicon mat or a sheet of baking paper will bring it together into a firm ball.

5 Wrap it in clingfilm then pop it into the fridge for 15 minutes.

Roll out the dough on a floured mat into the desired shape and about 1cm thick, using a second sheet of baking paper over the top.

(continued over page)

6 Remove the top sheet, then roll the mat or bottom piece of baking paper into a tube with the dough inside. Position the dough over the flan tin and unroll the tube, then gently press the pastry into the correct position in the tin, trying not to tear it. Prick the base of the pastry with a fork.

7 Cut off the excess dough by running a knife around the top, and patch up any tears with small pieces. (Use any leftover pastry to cut into biscuits or small shapes for decoration.) Bake for 25–30 minutes until golden. Leave to cool.

FOR THE VEGAN PASTRY

100g cassava flour

200g almond flour

2 tbsp coconut sugar or sweetener

2 tbsp psyllium husk

1 tsp gluten-free baking powder

4 tbsp olive oil, or avocado or coconut oil

1 tbsp vanilla extract

TRY SOMETHING DIFFERENT

These recipes work beautifully as simple vanilla biscuits. Make up the recipe and use a fun cookie cutter to create shapes. Bake for 10–15 minutes until golden brown.

1 Preheat the oven to 170°C (150°C fan oven) Gas 3. Grease a 23cm loose-based tart tin.

2 To make the vegan pastry, put all the ingredients into a food processor and blitz for a few seconds.

3 Pour in 125ml hot water and blend for a further few seconds until well mixed.

4 Using a silicon spatula, scrape the batter out into your hands and roll it into a ball until it has a play-dough-like texture (activating the psyllium husk).

5 Roll out the ball of dough between two sheets of baking paper into a disc about 1cm thick and wide enough to cover the circumference of the tart tin.

6 Remove the top layer of paper and lift the bottom sheet, then gently tip the pastry over the prepared flan tin. Don't press it in just yet.

7 Slowly peel off the paper, and ever so gently shape it into the tin, making sure to press it into the grooves around the edges and being careful to avoid tearing if possible. Trim around the edges with a knife, and use any excess dough to patch up any tears. (Use any leftover pastry to cut into biscuits or small stars for decoration.) Prick the base with a fork and bake for 25 minutes or until golden. Leave to cool in the tin.

1
RIEN QUE NOUS DEUX
VALSE
Sur les motifs de la célèbre chanson
EUGÈNE ROSI
Mouvt de Valse
INTROD.
EDITION UNIVERSELLE, 52, Faubg St Martin, Paris.
E 982 J.

I don't think I know any South African who would turn down a slice of this age-old South African classic, *melktert*. Although traditionally made with a sweet-crust pastry filled with a creamy custard of milk, flour, eggs and sugar, this version will definitely be kinder on the waistline, arteries and gut.

There are so many variations to making a traditional milk tart that are passed down through the generations. As this recipe is not a family secret, I'm delighted to share it with you.

MILK TART

DAIRY-FREE/GLUTEN-FREE/PALEO

SERVES 12

750ml canned full-fat coconut milk

3 tbsp coconut oil

3 egg yolks

2 tbsp cassava flour

2 tbsp tapioca flour or arrowroot powder

3–4 tbsp raw honey, to taste

2 tbsp powdered grass-fed gelatin or 1 tsp agar-agar

1 tsp almond extract, or to taste

2 tsp vanilla extract, or to taste

½ tsp freshly grated nutmeg (optional)

a sprinkle of ground cinnamon, to decorate

23cm pastry case (see page 199/200)

1 Pour 500ml of the coconut milk into a saucepan and add the coconut oil. Warm the mixture slowly over a medium-low heat until warm and starting to steam (you should still be able to stick your finger into the milk).

2 Put the remaining ingredients, including the remaining 250ml milk, in a bowl and whisk together.

3 Pour the egg mixture into the warmed milk over the heat, stirring constantly. Continue stirring or use a whisk while the custard thickens. Initially it will have a thin white layer of foam, which will start to settle down after a few minutes, and the custard will then start to become beautiful and shiny. Around this stage it will begin to thicken enough to coat the back of a spoon.

4 Taste it and decide if you like the flavour. Does it need more sweetener or extract? Add more if you prefer.

5 Once thickened, pour the mixture into the pastry case and transfer to the fridge for 2 hours or until set. Gently remove from the tart tin and dust with ground cinnamon before serving.

I'd love to be able to tell you how long this tart keeps for, but sadly it doesn't make it past a few hours in my house with my guys. This has got to be the most deliciously creamy lemony tart you will ever make, loaded with good healthy fats that will leave your family asking for a cheeky second (or third) slice.

LEMON TART

DAIRY-FREE/GLUTEN-FREE/PALEO

SERVES 12

80ml coconut oil

4 tbsp raw honey, or maple syrup or sweetener

125ml lemon juice

3 free-range eggs

125ml canned full-fat coconut milk

2 tsp powdered grass-fed gelatin or ½ tsp agar-agar

23cm pastry case (see page 199/200)

TIP

Strain the curd through a sieve if any eggy bits have formed. This will happen if the pan is too hot or the mixture is overcooked.

1 Melt the coconut oil and honey in a small saucepan over a very low heat, then add the lemon juice and whisk together.

2 In a bowl, whisk the eggs and coconut milk, then pour this into the warm lemon mixture. Turn the heat up to medium.

3 Continue stirring or use a whisk until the mixture starts to steam, then slowly and in small amounts sprinkle over the gelatin and continue to whisk it through. The mixture will thicken to the point when stirring it will leave tracks; this will take about 5 minutes. At this point remove from the heat and leave to cool until warm. Keep stirring occasionally to prevent a thick skin from forming.

4 Pour into the pastry case and transfer to the fridge for 1 hour to set.

As far as I'm concerned, chocolate and clementine (or orange) is the ultimate flavour pairing, and Kyra suggested that I create a recipe using these simple ingredients. In South Africa we call clementines *naartjies* (pronounced naar-chees) and it's a word that my girls have fun teaching to their friends here in the UK; the word *naartjie* rolls off the tongue as smoothly as this tart tastes.

I've used whole clementines, including the peel. Nope, I haven't gone crazy! The peel is not only loaded with fibre and vitamin C but it also contains oils that enhance the citrus flavour.

KYRA'S CHOCOLATE AND CLEMENTINE TART

DAIRY-FREE/GLUTEN-FREE/PALEO/VEGAN

SERVES 12

2 seedless clementines, unpeeled

400g canned full-fat coconut milk

160ml coconut cream

½ tsp agar-agar or 1 tsp powdered grass-fed gelatin

200g dairy-free dark chocolate chips

1 tsp orange extract (optional)

FOR THE CRUST

165g fresh Medjool dates, or dried unsweetened dates soaked in warm water until soft, pitted

100g ground almonds or almond flour

60ml coconut oil, melted, plus extra for greasing

3 tbsp raw cacao powder

1 tbsp vanilla extract

a pinch of pink salt

1 Start by boiling the clementines in a saucepan of water for 20 minutes, then remove them from the water and leave them to cool. Chop roughly (including the peel).

2 Preheat the oven to 170°C (150°C fan oven) Gas 3. Grease a loose-based tart tin.

3 To make the crust, put the crust ingredients into a food processor and blend to a dough-like consistency.

4 Using damp fingers, press the dough into the tart tin ensuring even thickness all over (make sure there are no holes in the crust or your filling will pour through). Bake for 15 minutes, then remove from the oven and leave to cool completely.

5 Put the chopped clementines into a blender and add the coconut milk and cream, then blitz until as smooth as possible. If there are few little bumps of clementine skin, don't worry, it won't be noticeable in the final product.

6 Pour the mixture into a saucepan and heat gently over a medium heat until it starts to steam.

7 Whisk through the agar-agar, then add the chocolate chips. Leave to stand for 5 minutes.

8 Whisk the chocolate mixture until well blended, and leave to cool slightly. Pour into the crust shell and leave to cool, then transfer to the fridge for 3 hours or until set.

Toby is a family friend who is both gluten and dairy intolerant, so he really enjoys being able to feast on puddings at our home. This pudding is his favourite, and his face lights up when he hears it is on the menu. A much-loved traditional English classic dessert, sticky date pudding really is the easiest fuss-free pudding and it is such a hit at a dinner party, not just with people who battle with intolerances, but with everyone. Ensure that you have a jar of the caramel sauce in the fridge; if not I suggest you make up a batch before baking the pudding.

TOBY'S STICKY DATE PUDDING

DAIRY-FREE/GLUTEN-FREE/PALEO

SERVES 4–6

200g fresh Medjool dates, or dried unsweetened dates, pitted and chopped

1 tsp bicarbonate of soda

2 tbsp blackstrap molasses

75g coconut oil, melted, plus extra for greasing

2 large free-range eggs

1 tbsp vanilla extract

100g ground almonds

50g cassava flour

2 tsp gluten-free baking powder

Salted Caramel Sauce, page 171, to top and serve

non-dairy ice cream, to serve

TIP

This dish can be made up a day in advance and then warmed in the oven before serving.

1 Preheat the oven to 180°C (160°C fan oven) Gas 4. Grease a baking dish thoroughly with coconut oil. Put the dates in a bowl and add the bicarbonate of soda, molasses and 200ml water. Stir together, then set aside to soften (this can be done well in advance).

2 Put the coconut oil in a bowl and add the eggs and vanilla extract. Whisk together until smooth.

3 Add the ground almonds, cassava flour and baking powder, and mix well using a wooden spoon, but don't beat it.

4 Stir the date mixture into the almond mixture until well combined. Transfer the batter to the baking dish and bake for 30–35 minutes until firm. Top with warmed caramel sauce and leave to stand for 5 minutes, allowing the sauce to soak into the pudding. Serve with ice cream and extra caramel sauce.

This recipe is one of the most popular recipes on my website. I created it for a chocolate campaign that I was doing at the time, and in all honesty, I didn't expect it to be such a hit. The original image went on to be shortlisted for the Pink Lady Food Photographer of the Year in 2017, which was a huge turning point in my photography career.

This pudding has gone through many changes and adaptations over the years – I've found that aubergine works best and adds a great steamed-pudding texture. Make this up a few days before Christmas and leave it in the fridge to develop in flavour. It will be a huge hit at the table, and your vegan family and friends will be blown away. Start preparations the day before.

VEGAN CHRISTMAS PUDDING

DAIRY-FREE/GLUTEN-FREE/PALEO/VEGAN

SERVES 12

250g mixed raisins, sultanas and cranberries

125ml brandy, or strong tea made with 1 teabag in 125ml water

200g aubergines, peeled and diced

100g Bramley or Granny Smith apples, cored and diced

150g fresh Medjool dates, or dried unsweetened dates soaked in warm water until soft, pitted and chopped

zest and juice of 1 large orange, plus extra if needed

1 tbsp vanilla extract

1 tsp almond extract

60ml coconut or olive oil, plus extra for greasing

100g almond flour

1 The day before, soak the raisins in the brandy in a bowl.

2 Boil or steam the aubergine and apple until very soft, then drain well and pat dry with kitchen paper.

3 Put the aubergine mixture in a food processor or blender and add the dates, zest and juice of the orange, the vanilla and almond extracts and the oil. Blitz to a purée, then set aside.

4 In a bowl measure out the almond flour, coconut flour, flaxseed, psyllium husk, cacao, coconut sugar, hemp seeds and spices, and mix well.

5 Combine the aubergine purée with the dry ingredients and mix well, adding more orange juice if needed.

6 Stir in the soaked raisins and any remaining brandy, and the nuts.

7 Grease a 1 litre Pyrex bowl or Christmas pudding bowl and fill with the mixture.

8 Cover with a circle of baking paper, then add a layer of foil over the paper and secure it tightly with string.

9 When ready to cook, put the bowl in a large saucepan on an upturned saucer. Fill the pan with enough hot water to reach three-quarters of the way up the bowl. Cover with a lid.

3 tbsp coconut flour

80g milled flaxseed

2 tbsp psyllium husk

3 tbsp raw cacao powder

100g coconut sugar

40g shelled hemp seeds

1 tbsp ground cinnamon

1 ½ tsp ground ginger

1 ½ tsp freshly grated nutmeg

½ tsp ground cloves

50g hazelnuts, chopped

100g pecan nuts, chopped

brandy, to serve

Salted Caramel Sauce (page 171), or White Chocolate Sauce (page 216) or Whipped Coconut Cream (page 173), to serve

TIP

It's quicker to cook this in an Instant Pot: cook for 45 minutes on 'manual' and allow the vent to drop completely before opening. Reheat for 10 minutes on 'manual', then remain on 'keep warm' until ready to serve.

10 Bring to the boil then reduce the heat to medium and gently boil the pudding for 3 hours.

11 Remove from the water and leave to cool. If you are making this up a few days beforehand, simply put the whole bowl, still covered, in the fridge until needed. To reheat, allow the pudding to return to room temperature, then use the same cooking method of hot water in a covered saucepan for 30 minutes or until warmed all the way through. Turn the bowl upside down and gently coax the pudding out of the bowl.

12 Flambé the pudding with warmed brandy and serve warm with caramel sauce, white chocolate sauce or whipped coconut cream.

My gorgeous friend Sue has a beautiful garden with a number of cooking-apple trees. Every September I love to pop past, grab a cuppa and have a good chat, then proceed to raid her apple trees.

Traditional recipes will tell you to remove the peel from your apples, but please don't, as the peel is incredibly nutritious and adds a boost of fibre and vitamin C to your dish. Obviously, being able to get your hands on some home-grown organic apples is first prize, but if you are unable to, just give your store-bought apples a good soak and a wash in bicarbonate of soda to remove any nasties. This not a particularly sweet dish, so if your family prefer a sweeter version, feel free to add raisins or a tablespoon or two of raw honey, maple syrup or coconut sugar to the apple mixture.

BRAMLEY APPLE CRUMBLE

DAIRY-FREE/GLUTEN-FREE/PALEO/VEGAN

SERVES 8

2 tbsp coconut oil, plus extra for greasing

750g Bramley apples (or Granny Smith or Pink Lady), unpeeled, cored and cut into chunks

juice of 1 small lemon

1 tsp ground cinnamon

1 tsp vanilla extract

FOR THE TOPPING

150g cassava flour

70g almond flour

125ml coconut oil (make sure it is cold and solid), cut into chunks

80g coconut sugar

45g flaked almonds

40g shelled hemp seeds

Whipped Coconut Cream (page 173) or Salted Caramel Sauce (page 171), or non-dairy ice cream, to serve

1 Preheat the oven to 170°C (150°C fan oven) Gas 3. Grease a baking dish. In a saucepan over a medium-high heat, melt the coconut oil and fry the apple chunks until they have a lovely golden caramelisation. If using cooking apples, don't push or stir them around too much: you want to keep them as solid as possible without breaking up.

2 Transfer to the prepared baking dish and squeeze over the lemon juice, then sprinkle over the cinnamon and vanilla extract, and give it a gentle stir (if you want to add extra sweetness, pop it in now).

3 To make the topping, put the cassava flour into a food processor and add the almond flour, chunks of coconut oil and coconut sugar, and pulse to create a breadcrumb texture.

4 Stir in the flaked almonds and hemp seeds. Sprinkle the mixture over the top of the apples, and bake for 40 minutes. Remove from the oven and serve warm with coconut cream or caramel sauce.

TIP

Make sure your coconut oil is cold and hard; this will ensure you get the crumble texture.

My husband, Derek, loves chocolate mousse; it's the first thing he will order for pudding in a restaurant, and I can honestly say that he considers himself a true connoisseur of all things chocolate mousse. Although I know that regular chocolate mousse is not that difficult to make, it still takes knowledge and experience to create the ultimate mousse, with a creamy and light texture. This recipe requires neither knowledge nor experience, and is a genuine showstopper for a night in front of the telly – or get posh and serve it at a dinner party.

THREE-INGREDIENT CHOCOLATE MOUSSE

DAIRY-FREE/GLUTEN-FREE/KETO/PALEO/VEGAN

MAKES 4

600ml canned full-fat coconut milk

1 tsp vanilla extract, or ½ tsp rosewater, orange or mint extract

250g dairy-free dark chocolate chips

1 Heat the coconut milk and vanilla extract in a saucepan over a medium heat until steaming.

2 Remove from the heat and add the chocolate chips. Don't stir – leave it to stand for 3 minutes.

3 Once the time is up, stir well and transfer to ramekins (or a piping bag) or a serving bowl. Cool then put in the fridge, uncovered, for a few hours until set. If using a piping bag, pipe the mousse into individual serving bowls or glasses.

I think this dish originated from The Ivy restaurant in London. We have enjoyed variations of it in a number of other restaurants, but we have never been lucky enough to find a dairy-free version on our travels, so I have made my own. It's a beautiful and exciting combination of hot and cold, sweet and tart, and it really gets the taste buds firing on all cylinders. Really, really easy to make, this definitely is a delight to serve to family and friends on hot summer evenings.

FROZEN SUMMER BERRIES WITH WHITE CHOCOLATE SAUCE

DAIRY-FREE/GLUTEN-FREE/KETO/PALEO/VEGAN

SERVES 4

700g frozen mixed summer berries

FOR THE WHITE CHOCOLATE SAUCE

250ml coconut cream

1 tbsp raw honey, or maple syrup or sweetener

1 tsp vanilla extract

30g raw cacao butter discs (they look like white chocolate; find them in health stores or on Amazon)

TIP

If you have really big berries, it's best to quickly blitz them through a food processor. Put them back in the freezer to chill before serving.

1 To make the white chocolate sauce, heat the cream, honey and vanilla in a saucepan over a medium heat until steaming.

2 Add the cacao butter and leave to stand for a few minutes.

3 Whisk well until the discs have melted. Either keep warm or set the saucepan aside to warm just before serving.

4 Spoon the frozen berries into individual bowls and top with the hot sauce.

'Growing market produce has been at the core of our business from the outset, and we firmly believe that freshly harvested vegetables and fruit are at the heart of a healthy, sustainable diet. We are proud to sell our own home-grown produce to our customers metres from where they are grown, on the day they are picked, knowing that they are at their very best.

Greg Secretts, managing director, Secretts Farm, PYO & Farm Shop, Milford, Surrey

This recipe fills me with such nostalgia, as it was the first recipe I ever photographed and put up on my website eighty20nutrition. It came about when I learned that cherries are great to help with insomnia because they are rich in melatonin. At that stage one of my family members was struggling with sleep, and we had a huge box of cherries from a summer trip to Brugge, so it seemed the perfect reason to create this recipe. Although I can't remember if it actually helped with the sleep, I do know that there is nothing more relaxing and soothing on a hot summer's night than a bowl of cherry ice cream.

CHERRY AND ROSE ICE CREAM

DAIRY-FREE/GLUTEN-FREE/KETO/PALEO/VEGAN

SERVES 8–10

1kg frozen pitted cherries (make life easy and buy frozen ones from the supermarket)

250ml coconut cream

1 tsp rosewater or a few drops of rose oil

juice of 1 plump lime

sweetener to taste (optional)

1 tbsp vodka (optional)

TIP

The vodka is optional and tasteless; it helps with the freezing process to prevent large icicles forming.

TRY SOMETHING DIFFERENT

Add a handful of dairy-free dark chocolate chips for extra crunch and flavour.

1 Put all the ingredients into a blender. Blitz until smooth and the consistency of ice cream.

2 Taste and adjust flavours if necessary. Transfer to a 450g metal loaf tin (it keeps it colder for longer when serving and has that authentic ice-cream-parlour look) and freeze for 4 hours.

We have a constant stash of frozen bananas in our freezer. Mainly because if a bunch doesn't get eaten, I'd rather peel and freeze them for ice cream, which I know will be devoured. Frozen banana is magical when blitzed through a food processor, as it transforms into the most amazingly smooth and creamy soft-serve ice-cream consistency. Topped with everyone's favourite, peanut butter, you really do have a winning combination.

PEANUT BUTTER AND BANANA ICE CREAM

DAIRY-FREE/GLUTEN-FREE/PALEO/VEGAN

SERVES 6–8

1kg bananas, peeled, chopped and frozen

125ml coconut cream

3 tbsp sugar-free peanut butter (or any other nut butter)

TIP

Substitute the peanut butter with Salted Caramel Sauce (page 171).

1 Remove the bag of frozen bananas from the freezer, then drop the bag on the kitchen counter or floor to break up the individual pieces inside.

2 Put the pieces in a food processor and add the coconut cream. Run the processor until the banana is smooth and a soft-serve consistency.

3 Mix the peanut butter with 1–2 tbsp boiling water to make it slightly runny.

4 Pour the ice cream into a cake tin or loaf tin lined with baking paper or a freezerproof container, and drizzle the peanut butter over the top. Return to the freezer for 1 hour. If it's in the freezer for longer and becomes difficult to serve, just leave it to stand to soften it.

Deliciously refreshing and creamy, these adult ice lollies really get the taste buds firing. Feel free to swap the rum for rum essence, or even just leave it out for a healthy afternoon snack for kids. I generally like to add a touch of alcohol to my lollies and ice cream because it slows down the freezing process and stops them from becoming one big ice block.

PINA COLADA POPSICLES

DAIRY-FREE/GLUTEN-FREE/PALEO/VEGAN

MAKES 8

700g fresh pineapple, skinned and chopped

juice of 1 lime

160ml coconut cream

3–4 tbsp rum, to taste (optional)

1 Put all the ingredients in a blender and blitz together, then pour into eight ice-lolly moulds. Freeze overnight.

I have such happy childhood memories of playing in the swimming pool and hearing the ice-cream man ringing his bell from the street. We'd beg mum for money and run barefoot after him in the hope of getting to him before he rode away. Chocolate ice lollies were the prize – as we peered into the big cooler box attached to the front of his bike, they were the first ones we'd look for. Sadly, my girls will never know that kind of life that I lived growing up in Zimbabwe, but I can recreate a special taste from my childhood to share with them: rich, chocolatey and fudgy, I'd go as far as to say that these are even better than the ones from my childhood.

FUDGY CHOCOLATE ICE LOLLIES

DAIRY-FREE/GLUTEN-FREE/KETO/PALEO/VEGAN

MAKES 8

400ml canned full-fat coconut milk

250ml canned coconut cream

4 tbsp coconut sugar

1 tbsp tapioca flour

1 tbsp instant coffee powder

2 tbsp raw cacao powder

2 tsp vanilla extract

a pinch of pink salt, or to taste

80g dark dairy-free chocolate chips

1½ tsp vodka (optional)

TIP

The vodka is tasteless; it is added to prevent large ice crystals forming in the ice cream, keeping it smooth and silky.

1 In a saucepan, combine the coconut milk, coconut cream, coconut sugar, tapioca flour, coffee, cacao, vanilla and salt. Heat the mixture over a medium heat until it starts to steam.

2 Remove from the heat and sprinkle in the chocolate chips and vodka, if using. Don't stir yet; just leave it to stand for 3 minutes, then give it a good stir.

3 Pour the chocolate mixture into eight ice-lolly moulds and freeze for a minimum of 4 hours.

A Healthier Family for Life | Bakes, Puddings & Snacks

We went through a really tough exam period in our house a few years ago. Anyone who has had children doing both A-levels and GCSEs at the same time will know that your home feels smothered by a huge exam blanket. As a mother, there is nothing worse than that helpless feeling of watching your children exhaustedly tackle the books, so I tried to ease the pain by making up endless batches of these brownies for much-needed tea and snacks, all served with a few motherly hugs.

FUDGY DARK CHOCOLATE BROWNIES

DAIRY-FREE/GLUTEN-FREE/PALEO

MAKES 20

250g fresh Medjool dates, or dried unsweetened dates, pitted and finely chopped

1 tsp bicarbonate of soda

3 free-range eggs, at room temperature

125ml nut milk

1 heaped tbsp tahini or nut butter

250g ground almonds

50g dark unsweetened cocoa or raw cacao powder

1 tsp gluten-free baking powder

100g dark dairy-free chocolate chips or chopped nuts

1 Preheat the oven to 170°C (150°C fan oven) Gas 3. Line a traybake/brownie tin with baking paper or, even better, use a silicon one if possible.

2 Put the dates in a bowl with 200ml hot water and sprinkle over the bicarbonate of soda. Mix well and then set aside to cool.

3 In a food processor, blend the eggs, milk and tahini.

4 Strain the cooled dates, then add them to the egg mixture and blitz for 1 minute until smooth. Add the ground almonds, cocoa and baking powder, and blend for just 1–2 seconds until mixed.

5 Stir in half the dark chocolate chips. Transfer the batter to the prepared traybake tin and sprinkle with the remaining chocolate chips. Bake for 25–30 minutes until they feel firm when pressed (avoid touching any of the chocolate because it gets super-hot). Remove from the oven and leave to cool, then slice into 20 squares and enjoy.

When packing lunch boxes or snacks for school, it can be a challenge keeping them nut-free to adhere to school regulations. I was so excited when I nailed this recipe, because not only is it just the easiest to whip up, but they also taste great and are filling, which really helps with a mid-morning school snack.

LUNCH BOX CHOCOLATE MUFFINS

DAIRY-FREE/GLUTEN-FREE/KETO/PALEO

MAKES 6

3 free-range eggs

60ml coconut oil

3 tbsp maple syrup, or raw honey or sweetener

2 tsp vanilla extract

1 tsp raw apple cider vinegar

4 tbsp coconut flour

4 tbsp raw cacao powder

½ tsp pink salt

1 tsp gluten-free baking powder

50g dark dairy-free chocolate chips (optional for a more chocolatey flavour)

½ tsp mint or rose extract (optional for a varied flavour)

1 Preheat the oven to 180°C (160°C fan oven) Gas 4. Line a muffin tray with 6 small paper cupcake cases or small muffin cups. Put all the ingredients in a bowl and mix together well.

2 Divide the mixture evenly among the muffin cups. Bake for 20–25 minutes until raised and firm. Cool on a wire rack.

In keeping with my South African heritage, this book would not be complete without sharing a recipe for rusks. A true South African rusk is a twice-baked biscuit – first baked in cake form, then cut up and left to dry out slowly at a low temperature until crispy. Served with a cup of tea or coffee, and then dunked, these rusks are delicious. It is all in the timing of the dunk, however: leave it in too long and the rusk will become soggy and break off. Many a childhood has been spent calculating the perfect dunking time, but if all else fails, a teaspoon to scoop out the bits from the bottom is all that is needed.

Originating in the 1690s, rusks were a way of preserving bread and were used during the Great Trek and Boer Wars. Today, they are perfect for an on-the-go brekkie, or for camping or a long car journey.

MUESLI RUSKS

DAIRY-FREE/GLUTEN-FREE/KETO/PALEO

MAKES 28

3 free-range eggs

1 tbsp vanilla extract

1 tsp almond extract (optional but adds a beautiful flavour)

125ml coconut oil, melted

400g tin full-fat coconut milk

1 tbsp raw apple cider vinegar

125ml raw honey, or maple syrup, 100g coconut sugar or sweetener

200g almond flour or ground almonds

40g coconut flour

30g tapioca flour

50g milled flaxseed (or almond flour)

1 tbsp psyllium husk

50g desiccated coconut

1 Preheat the oven to 180°C (160°C fan oven) Gas 4. Prepare a 35cm rectangular traybake tin or roasting tin with baking paper (I use a rectangular roasting tin 7cm deep to allow for rising).

2 Put the eggs in a large bowl and add the vanilla and almond extracts, the oil, milk, vinegar and honey. Whisk together until light and fluffy.

3 In another bowl combine the remaining ingredients and stir until well mixed. Add the dry ingredients to the wet ingredients and mix well.

4 Spoon the batter into the prepared tin and spread it out evenly. Bake for 40 minutes until golden brown and firm in the middle – a gentle prod with your finger will do the test.

5 Remove from the oven and turn the oven down to 80°C (70°C fan oven) or the lowest possible gas mark and leave the door slightly ajar.

6 Lift the paper and the cake out of the baking tray and leave on a wire rack to cool for 10 minutes.

7 Cut into 10 x 4cm rusks. Line the rusks up on an oven rack or shelf (see Tip), leaving a small space between each rusk. Bake them slowly, for a minimum of 4 hours, but ideally overnight for a really dry, crisp rusk. Turn off the oven and leave them inside to cool completely. Store in an airtight container.

1 tbsp bicarbonate of soda

1 tbsp ground cinnamon

2 tsp freshly grated nutmeg

1 tsp ground ginger

100g flaked almonds

100g hazelnuts, chopped

100g pecan nuts, chopped

200g raisins or dried cranberries

100g pumpkin seeds

100g sunflower seeds

TIP

An oven rack or shelf is the adjustable shelf that comes with your oven. It is a stainless steel grid and perfect for allowing the air to circulate around the entire rusk while it dries out completely.

TRY SOMETHING DIFFERENT

This is a pretty durable recipe and the nuts and seeds can be substituted for any others that you might have in your cupboard or that you prefer; feel free to play around with different nuts and flavours.

I recently heard about a type of biscuit called a muffin top. Think of the delicious crispy top of the muffin – you know, the top bit that overflows from the paper cup. (I always pull it off first and save it for last.) Well, these biscuits are just like that: crispy on the outside, soft on the inside and loaded with chunks of melted chocolate.

CHUNKY CHOC-CHIP COOKIES

DAIRY-FREE/GLUTEN-FREE/KETO/PALEO

MAKES 15

2 free-range eggs

125ml coconut oil, melted

4 tbsp coconut sugar

2 tsp vanilla extract

300g almond flour or ground almonds

½ tsp gluten-free baking powder

a pinch of pink salt

50g dark dairy-free chocolate chips

1 Preheat the oven to 170°C (150°C fan oven) Gas 3. Line a baking sheet with either a silicon mat or baking paper. Put the eggs in a bowl and add the oil, coconut sugar and vanilla extract. Whisk together.

2 Stir in the almond flour, baking powder, salt and chocolate chips.

3 Using a small ice-cream scoop, evenly scoop out balls of the dough and put them on the prepared baking sheet, leaving space all round each one.

4 Using a wet fork, ever so slightly push down the top, not too much though. Bake for 18–20 minutes until golden. Leave to cool on the baking sheet until firm, then transfer to a wire rack to cool completely.

These truffles are ideal for lunchboxes or as an afternoon snack, and they also make beautiful and thoughtful gifts. My family have learned to question everything that I ask them to taste, I guess it comes from years of 'Here, try this ...', only to discover that it contained a hidden healthy ingredient. Getting these truffles with hidden avocado past their hound-dog noses was a challenge that I set myself – and I'll have you know, they passed with flying colours.

AVOCADO AND ALMOND TRUFFLES

DAIRY-FREE/GLUTEN-FREE/KETO/PALEO/VEGAN

MAKES 20

350g ripe avocado flesh

100g almond butter

4 tbsp coconut oil, melted

4 tbsp raw honey, or maple syrup or powdered sweetener

4 tbsp raw cacao powder

½ tsp pink salt

1 tbsp vanilla extract

½ tsp almond extract

desiccated coconut, or chopped nuts or a topping of your choice, for rolling

1 Put all the ingredients, except the coconut for rolling, into a food processor or blender and blitz together until smooth.

2 Pour the mixture into a rectangular plastic or glass container and chill in the fridge for 2 hours or until firm.

3 Dampen your hands then, using a small ice-cream scoop or a 1 tbsp measuring spoon, scoop out balls and roll them between your hands.

4 Roll the balls in desiccated coconut to finish them off. Store in the fridge for up to 1 week.

Marzipan is like Marmite: you either love it or hate it. The addition of cacao butter not only adds a delicious taste but it is also really healthy. It's great for giving you a head of shiny hair, and it also boosts the immune function and metabolism, and is loaded with saturated fats for brain function.

These sweets take so little time to make up and are perfect for an after-dinner treat, a lunchbox snack or a gorgeous homemade Christmas present for a marzipan-loving friend.

DARK CHOCOLATE MARZIPAN BALLS

DAIRY-FREE/GLUTEN-FREE/KETO/PALEO/VEGAN

MAKES 12

25g cacao butter drops

200g almond flour

2 tbsp raw honey or maple syrup

1 tsp almond extract

200g dairy-free dark chocolate

1 tsp coconut oil

TIP

For cooling the chocolate-coated balls, you can also put an orange inside a ramekin, then use a cocktail stick for each ball and stick each into the orange to allow the balls to set without pooling.

1 Melt the cacao butter drops in a heatproof bowl over a pan of gently simmering water or on a low heat setting in a microwave.

2 Put the almond flour in a food processor or blender and add the melted cacao butter, 60ml water, the honey and vanilla extract, and blend to a paste consistency.

3 Roll the mixture into balls and put them in the fridge to firm up for 1 hour (or use the freezer if in a hurry).

4 Melt the chocolate and coconut oil in a heatproof bowl over a pan of gently simmering water, stirring occasionally. (Alternatively, using a microwaveable bowl: melt the dark chocolate and coconut oil in the microwave for two or three 30-second intervals, stirring in between.)

5 Cover a baking sheet with baking paper (or see Tip below). Remove the balls from the fridge. Use a cocktail stick to pierce the ball, and dunk the entire ball into the chocolate, then hover it over the bowl to allow the excess to run off.

6 Put the ball on the prepared baking sheet, remove the stick and continue with the others. Leave to cool, and enjoy.

This is one of Derek's favourite treats, especially to help him stay in keto or to push him into keto, which requires the diet to be low in carbohydrates and high in fat. I remember when I first made this many, many years ago. I called it fudge, and you can imagine the disappointment when it turned out to be nothing like the sweet sugary treat that the family had grown up with. It does take a while for your taste buds to change and not crave sweet sugar, but have faith that it will happen. Having a stash of these in the freezer really does help with those late-afternoon hunger crashes or cravings that get you reaching for something chewy or crispy.

WALNUT FAT BOMBS

DAIRY-FREE/GLUTEN-FREE/KETO/PALEO/VEGAN

MAKES 36

150g walnuts

200g light tahini

125ml coconut oil

30g raw cacao powder

2 tsp vanilla extract

1 tbsp raw honey, or maple syrup or sweetener

a pinch of pink salt

TIP

You must keep them stored in the freezer or fridge at all times.

1 Blitz the walnuts in a food processor or chop them into grain-sized crumbs.

2 Put a saucepan over a medium-low heat and heat the tahini and coconut oil together, then whisk in the remaining ingredients.

3 Stir in the nuts, then pour the mixture into small ice-cube trays or silicon chocolate moulds. Put the trays in the freezer and leave to set. You can keep the fat bombs in the trays and just pop one out whenever the craving hits.

I'm a huge fan of grass-fed gelatin. This is not the type of gelatine that you find in the baking section of the supermarket, but rather a purer, superior quality of gelatin that is purchased from a health store or online. It comes in a fine powder form and it is very light and dissolves easily in hot water. I initially had a fear of working with it, but the trick is to work quickly and whisk in small amounts at a time.

I have also made this recipe with agar-agar, but they just don't have the same chewy texture as the gelatin version. If you are accustomed to agar-agar in desserts, it's a similar result.

You might want to add extra flavour in the form of a few drops of extract or sweetener, because once the gelatin sets, the flavour will diminish slightly.

GUT-HEALING GUMMIES

DAIRY-FREE/GLUTEN-FREE/KETO/PALEO/VEGAN

MAKES 200 JELLY BABIES OR 18 2.5CM CUBES

250ml fresh orange juice or any other flavour

2 tbsp local raw honey or sweetener to taste, if needed

1 tsp orange extract

4 tbsp powdered grass-fed gelatin or 1 tbsp agar-agar for vegans

TIPS

Play around with different flavours; I've been known to use a multitude of different drinks, ranging from kombucha to coconut milk, in my years of making these. Once you get the hang of making these they really can be so much fun to mix and match flavour batches.

Amazon have a great selection of silicon moulds: anything from teddy bears to snakes. You will need about 4 jelly-baby trays and a pipette. If you use a silicon loaf tin, simply cut the mixture up to your preferred size.

1 Make sure you have your silicon mould ready and waiting; this can either be a gummy bear mould, chocolate moulds, ice-cube trays or even a silicon loaf tin.

2 Put the juice in a small saucepan over a medium heat and add the honey and extract. Heat through until the steam starts to rise, then slowly sprinkle in very small amounts of gelatin at a time, whisking in each addition. If you add too much at a time, it will clump.

3 Once all the gelatin has been whisked in and there are no clumps, pour the mixture into the moulds and transfer to the fridge to cool and set.

4 Remove from the moulds, or cut into 2.5cm cubes, and store in the fridge in an airtight container.

We are fortunate in having an incredible farm around the corner from where we live. They grow many amazing fruits and vegetables and have a farm shop on the property. During the summer they have pick-your-own strawberries, which is always the highlight of the season for us. There is something so primal about going into the fields and choosing your own food to forage. Although it's great to take the kids or visiting friends to pick their own strawberries, I always end up with a ton of berries and no idea what to do with them. Fruit leathers are fab for using any surplus fruit instead of wasting it.

STRAWBERRY FRUIT LEATHERS

DAIRY-FREE/GLUTEN-FREE/PALEO/VEGAN

MAKES 13

450g strawberries, hulled

2 tbsp raw honey or maple syrup (optional)

1 tbsp lemon juice

1 tsp vanilla extract, or more if needed

TIPS

If you live in a hot climate, you can leave the leather in the sun to dry out, just ensure that you create a tent of netting over the tray to cover it.

Double the recipe and use two baking trays, just swap the trays around in the oven during drying.

1 Preheat the oven to 80°C (60°C fan oven) or the lowest possible gas mark and leave the door slightly ajar. Line a 35 x 25cm baking tray with baking paper or, ideally, a silicon sheet. Put the ingredients in a blender and blitz to a purée.

2 Taste the purée and decide if it needs any more flavour.

3 Heat the fruit purée in a saucepan over a medium heat until it starts to thicken slightly. You want a consistent bubble for about 15 minutes.

4 Transfer the purée to the prepared baking tray and spread it as thinly as possible. Put it in the oven to dry for 3–4 hours. It's ready when it is no longer sticky to the touch. This can take longer depending on your oven and how thick the mixture is.

5 Leave to cool, then cut into 2.5cm strips. Roll up and store in the fridge for up to 2 weeks.

Crunchy chocolate, gooey date caramel and salty peanuts – this recipe hits all the taste senses with a big punch.

CARAMEL, BISCUIT AND NUT BARS

DAIRY-FREE/GLUTEN-FREE/PALEO/VEGAN

MAKES 12

FOR THE BISCUIT BASE

100g almond flour

2 tbsp coconut flour

1 tbsp coconut sugar

a pinch of pink salt

1 tsp vanilla extract

1 tsp psyllium husk

1 tbsp avocado oil, or olive oil or coconut oil

FOR THE CARAMEL FILLING

150g fresh Medjool dates, or dried unsweetened dates, pitted and chopped

200g sugar-free chunky peanut butter (or nut butter of choice)

1 tsp vanilla extract

½ tsp pink salt

60g peanuts or tree nuts of choice

FOR THE CHOCOLATE TOPPING

200g dairy-free dark chocolate chips

1 tsp coconut oil

1 Preheat the oven to 170°C (150°C fan oven) Gas 3 and line a 450g loaf tin with baking paper. Put all the ingredients for the base in a bowl and add 2 tbsp water. Mix together well then transfer to the prepared baking tin.

2 Using the back of a spoon or a measuring cup, press the mixture down hard and flat, ensuring that the top is smooth and level. Bake for 20 minutes. Remove from the oven and leave to cool in the tin.

3 To make the filling, soak the dates in 250ml hot water for 10 minutes or until very soft.

4 Put the dates and liquid in a food processor or blender and add the peanut butter, vanilla and salt, then blitz until smooth. Add the peanuts and pulse until chopped to your preferred size (alternatively, you might prefer to keep them whole).

5 Spoon the caramel mixture over the cooled biscuit base. Level the top with the back of a spoon or measuring cup, then transfer to the fridge for 2 hours to cool.

6 To make the chocolate topping, melt the chocolate and coconut oil in a heatproof bowl over a pan of gently simmering water (or use a microwave), until smooth and runny. Pour over the top of the caramel. Swirl the tin around to ensure even distribution and put back in the fridge to set for 20 minutes.

7 Lift the baking paper and biscuit out of the tin, and slice into 12 even-sized bars (it's very rich, so only small slices are necessary).

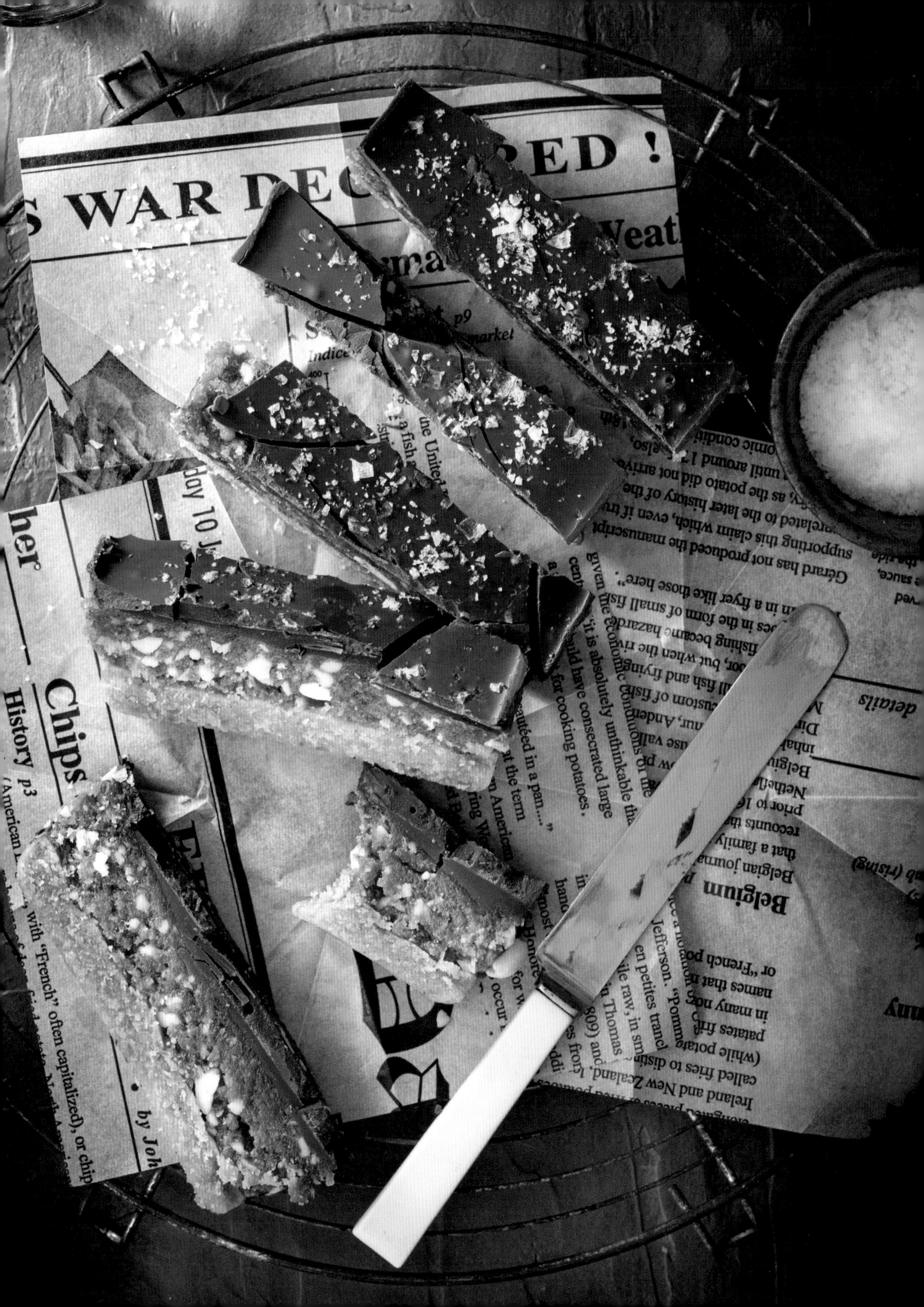
S WAR DEC
RED !
Chips
History p3
Belgium
details

To me coconut really is a superfood, loaded with incredible fats, rich in fibre, vitamins and minerals. My family love to tease me, because coconut is my go-to for anything and fixes everything in my home, from a squeaky kitchen door hinge to a sore throat.

COCONUT BARS

DAIRY-FREE/GLUTEN-FREE/KETO/PALEO/VEGAN

MAKES 6

120g desiccated coconut

125ml coconut cream

2–3 tbsp coconut sugar, or raw honey or sweetener, to taste

½ tsp vanilla extract

100g dark chocolate dairy-free chips

1 tsp coconut oil

TIP

Feel free to leave the chocolate out, they are delicious cut into squares like coconut ice.

1 Put the desiccated coconut in a bowl and add the coconut cream, sugar and vanilla extract. Mix together well.

2 Line the inside of a rectangular plastic food container (16 x 10cm) with clingfilm.

3 Transfer the coconut mixture to the container and press it down hard and tight, ensuring that the top is flat and even.

4 Chill in the fridge for 30 minutes – not too long, because it still needs to be soft enough to cut.

5 Remove from the fridge and cut into six even-sized bars using a very sharp knife, then reshape it to make chocolate-bar shapes. Freeze for 2 hours.

6 Melt the chocolate and coconut oil in a heatproof bowl over a pan of gently simmering water (or use a microwave). Lay a piece of baking paper on the work surface.

7 Using a cocktail stick, pierce the end of one bar and stand the bar on the opposite end in the chocolate. Using a spoon, scoop the chocolate up and over the bar until the entire bar is covered, then hold it up, allowing the chocolate to drip off.

8 Transfer to the baking paper and start again with a new cocktail stick and bar.

9 Once the chocolate has hardened, remove the cocktail sticks and store in the fridge for up to 2 weeks.

Green bananas are a good source of resistant starch – a type of starch that isn't fully broken down and absorbed by your body during the time of digestion. It easily travels through your stomach and small intestine undigested, eventually reaching your colon where it feeds your friendly gut bacteria. The fibre-rich content of green bananas is good for constipation and helping your digestive system to get back on track. Green bananas are safe to eat, although you might find them tougher to peel than yellow bananas. They also have a firmer texture and are not as sweet. Choose your bananas according to what you think is best for your family.

FRIED GREEN BANANA SUSHI

DAIRY-FREE/GLUTEN-FREE/KETO/PALEO/VEGAN

MAKES 24 SLICES

4 green bananas (or as ripe as your family prefers)

4 tbsp almond flour

4 tbsp desiccated coconut

4 tbsp coconut sugar or sweetener (optional)

½ tsp ground cinnamon

1 egg or 40ml nut milk

2–3 tbsp coconut oil, as needed for shallow frying

melted dairy-free dark chocolate, or Salted Caramel Sauce (page 171) or Whipped Coconut Cream (page 173), to serve

1 Peel and slice the bananas into 2.5cm chunks. Put the almond flour in a small mixing bowl, and add the coconut, cinnamon and coconut sugar. Combine well.

2 In another small bowl whisk the egg or pour in the nut milk. Heat the coconut oil in a frying pan over a medium-high heat.

3 Start by dipping the banana slices in egg (or milk) then into the flour mixture and then put them into the hot pan. Fry until crisp and golden on all sides.

4 Serve with melted chocolate, caramel sauce or coconut cream for dipping.

For some reason seeded gluten-free crackers in the supermarket are so ridiculously expensive, which totally dumbfounds me. When making them at home the ingredients are relatively inexpensive and I can make up a huge portion. Since I'm actually a chip-and-dip gal, having these crackers around really helps when the chip craving strikes. They are delicious served with Mackerel Pâté (page 148) and Kombucha Pickled Red Onion (page 159).

Use this recipe as a base for adding flavour, such as a handful of dried cranberries and cinnamon, or crushed walnuts and herbs.

MIXED SEED CRACKERS

DAIRY-FREE/GLUTEN-FREE/KETO/PALEO/VEGAN

MAKES 48

250g mixed seeds, such as sunflower, sesame and pumpkin

50g flaxseed

50g desiccated coconut

3 tbsp psyllium husk

½ tsp herbal salt (Herbamare)

2 tbsp avocado oil or melted coconut oil

500ml water or bone broth

TIP

If the centre of the biscuit mixture is a little thick and does not bake properly, simply break off the crisp pieces and pop the softer pieces back into the oven set to 110°C (90°C fan oven) Gas ¼ with the door slightly ajar until crispy.

1 Preheat the oven to 170°C (140°C fan oven) Gas 3. Line a baking tray with a silicon mat or reusable non-stick baking sheets (don't use paper as it is difficult to separate from the crackers once cooked).

2 Put all the dry ingredients in a large bowl and stir to mix.

3 Pour in the oil and water, mix well and then leave to stand for 5 minutes to activate the psyllium husk for thickening.

4 Transfer the batter to the prepared baking tray and spread it out as evenly and thinly as possible. Bake for 1 hour and 15 minutes, turning the tray around once during baking. They should be crisp and dark golden, if they aren't then pop them back into the oven, even turning the oven up slightly, keeping an eye on them the whole time.

5 Leave to cool and cut into 5cm squares or just break into pieces. Store in an airtight container for up to 1 month.

Salty, crispy and just so delicious, these chips are perfect to make for a road trip to help keep the junk-food snacking to a minimum. Serve with a side of guacamole to balance the saltiness, and this high-protein snack will keep the internal motors running for ages.

ROAD-TRIP PROSCIUTTO CHIPS

DAIRY-FREE/GLUTEN-FREE/KETO/PALEO

MAKES 10

10 slices of prosciutto

1 Preheat the oven to 220°C (200°C fan oven) Gas 7. Line a baking tray with baking paper. Lay the prosciutto onto the prepared baking tray (don't crowd them – they need space to crisp).

2 Bake for 7–9 minutes until the sides start to curl up. Remove and leave to cool. If your oven is not big enough to handle the whole load, bake them in batches using the same baking paper.

Having endured many exam seasons, I know how hard-working brains need constant refuelling with snacks – the healthy kind. These nuts are my exam-season speciality; I make them up by the truckload because my girls can never get enough of them. They can be made spicy, as with this recipe, or add a sweeter twist by using coconut sugar and ground cinnamon.

SPICED NUTS

DAIRY-FREE/GLUTEN-FREE/KETO/PALEO/VEGAN

MAKES 400G

400g cashew nuts or nuts of choice

2 tbsp avocado oil or melted coconut oil

1 tsp pink salt

½ tsp onion granules

½ tsp Italian herbs

½ tsp chilli powder (optional)

1 Preheat the oven to 200°C (180°C fan oven) Gas 6. Line a baking tray with baking paper. Put the nuts in a bowl and add the oil and flavourings.

2 Transfer to the prepared baking tray and spread them out evenly. Bake for 20–25 minutes until golden and toasty, stirring on a regular basis. Cool and store in an airtight container.

I often have massive salt cravings, and find myself reaching for a packet of crisps. Although I'm a self-confessed chip-aholic, I really have to fight the addiction and reach for something a little healthier, like these kale crisps. Large kale leaves are ideal for making them. Just remove the tough stem (give the stem to your dog – our Jack loves to eat them) and cut the leaves into crisp sizes, then sprinkle with spice, then a quick roast is easy enough to ensure that I can still have my crisp fix.

KALE CRISPS

DAIRY-FREE/GLUTEN-FREE/KETO/PALEO/VEGAN

MAKES 1 LARGE BOWL

150g kale leaves
1 tbsp avocado oil
½ tsp onion granules
½ tsp pink salt

1 Preheat the oven to 180°C (160°C fan oven) Gas 4 and line a baking tray or two with baking paper. Cut out and discard the middle stem from the leaves, and cut the leaves into crisp sizes. Put them into a bowl.

2 Drizzle the oil over the leaves and sprinkle with the onion granules and salt, then massage the oil and flavourings into the leaves to ensure a full covering.

3 Lay the leaves on the prepared baking tray, ensuring that they don't overlap. Bake for 10–15 minutes until the edges are brown but not burnt (keep watching them, as they can burn quickly). Leave to cool. They will crisp up when cooled.

What has happened to the age-old tradition of making popcorn and then sitting down to watch a movie? Nowadays we either rip open a packet of store-bought popcorn, or, even worse, a bag of MSG- and chemical-ridden microwave popcorn. Even though I didn't grow up in a home where cooking featured much, I still have amazing memories of making popcorn with my mum. There is just something so incredibly satisfying about sitting down to a bowl of fresh, homemade popcorn.

CHEESY DAIRY-FREE POPCORN

DAIRY-FREE/GLUTEN-FREE/KETO/PALEO/VEGAN

MAKES 1 BOWLFUL

3 tbsp avocado oil

80g popcorn kernels

FOR THE CHEESE-FLAVOURED TOPPING

3 tbsp nutritional yeast flakes

1 tsp pink salt

1 tsp paprika

1 Put the oil in a large heavy-based saucepan and add the popcorn kernels. Give it a good shake to cover the kernels in oil.

2 Cover the pan, then heat over a medium-high heat. While the popcorn is popping, make the topping. In a small bowl mix together the ingredients, then set aside.

3 Once the kernels have popped, remove the saucepan from the heat and sprinkle the popcorn with the topping, giving it a good shake to distribute it. Transfer to a serving bowl and enjoy with a good classic movie.

Drinks

The traditional way of making a shrub is by adding equal quantities of water and sugar to fruit and then vinegar to help preserve it. I have adapted this age-old recipe to keep it as low in sugar as possible. The healing properties of ginger and apple cider vinegar make this drink a must for every family member all year round, to keep the immune system strong. I also like to source local raw honey, which helps with Gemma's summer hay-fever attacks.

Be warned: I have not been shy with the ginger, as I love the strong, burning taste of a good ginger drink. This means that it should be treated as a cordial and is totally delicious topped with sparkling water or hot water as a tea.

GINGER SHRUB

DAIRY-FREE/GLUTEN-FREE/KETO/PALEO/VEGAN

MAKES 1 LARGE JAR

500g fresh ginger, unpeeled

1.25 litres filtered water

250ml raw apple cider vinegar

4 tbsp raw honey or a high-quality maple syrup

TIP

Make it keto by leaving out the honey, or use a preferred sweetener.

1 Roughly chop the ginger. Put all the ingredients in a large saucepan, cover with a lid and bring to the boil, then reduce the heat and gently simmer over a low heat for 2–3 hours (you could also use a slow cooker or an Instant Pot).

2 Strain the shrub through a muslin cloth or a fine sieve, and pour into a glass jar. Cool, then chill in the fridge and use within 3 weeks.

Why mylk and not milk? Milk is from animals and mylk is from plants, which makes sense, so anyone who is vegan can instantly recognise the origin of their drink.

Why pumpkin seeds and not the regular nut mylk? Pumpkin seeds are not only much cheaper to purchase but also the mylk is incredibly delicious. It's also really nutritious, containing high levels of magnesium, which is generally lacking in the average Western diet.

Any kind of mylk-making is a process of love, but it is also incredibly satisfying and yields a fair amount, which can also be frozen for later use.

PUMPKIN SEED MYLK

DAIRY-FREE/GLUTEN-FREE/KETO/PALEO/VEGAN

MAKES 1 LITRE

200g pumpkin seeds

1 litre filtered water, plus extra for soaking

TIP

Give the mylk a good stir or shake before use, as separation occurs when left standing.

1 Put the pumpkin seeds in a bowl with enough filtered water to cover them, then cover and leave to stand for between 12 and 24 hours.

2 Drain the water, then rinse the seeds. Put them into a blender or food processor.

3 Add 1 litre fresh filtered water and blend to a pulp.

4 Strain the pumpkin water through a muslin cloth or nut bag, squeezing out as much liquid as possible. Pour into a jug or bottle and store in the fridge for up to 5 days.

Loaded with deliciously healthy fats, this hot chocolate is almost a meal in a mug. I like to add a few dark chocolate chips for extra pleasure, but feel free to leave them out and serve this as a meal replacement for anyone convalescing or for an 'I'm just not that hungry' kind of meal.

NOURISHING HOT CHOCOLATE

DAIRY-FREE/GLUTEN-FREE/KETO/PALEO/VEGAN

SERVES 2-4

400ml canned full-fat coconut milk

125ml nut milk

3 tbsp raw cacao powder

a pinch of pink salt

honey, or maple syrup or sweetener, to taste

1 egg yolk (optional)

a dash of vanilla extract, or rose or mint extract

50g dairy-free dark chocolate chips (optional)

1 Put all the ingredients, except the chocolate chips, in a saucepan and whisk well.

2 Gently warm over a medium heat until steaming.

3 If using chocolate chips, add them now and allow the mixture to stand undisturbed for 1–2 minutes until the chocolate has melted, then whisk well. Pour into mugs and serve.

My family calls this 'Christmas in a bottle', and no matter what time of the year it brings happiness to those who drink it. Add the concentrate to ice cold mylk (page 265) or a splash in a cup of tea.

ROOIBOS CHAI CONCENTRATE

DAIRY-FREE/GLUTEN-FREE/KETO/PALEO/VEGAN

MAKES 1 LITRE

1 litre filtered water

5 rooibos (redbush) tea bags

a thumb-sized piece of fresh ginger, unpeeled and sliced

3 large cinnamon sticks, broken in half

1 tbsp whole cloves

1 tbsp cardamom pods, slightly crushed

the peel of 1 whole orange or clementine peel, sliced

1 tbsp vanilla extract

1 Put all the ingredients in a large saucepan over a high heat and bring to the boil, then turn off the heat and leave to infuse for 10 minutes.

2 Remove the teabags and leave to cool in the fridge overnight.

3 Strain the mixture through a fine sieve or muslin cloth, and transfer the chai concentrate to a sterile glass bottle for storage. Use within 3 weeks.

TIPS

To sterilise bottles and jars, put washed bottles in the dishwasher on a full cycle. Or wash and rinse thoroughly, then put upturned on a baking sheet in the oven at 140°C (120°C fan oven) Gas 1 for 10–15 minutes. Or put them on a trivet in the Instant Pot, use 250ml water and set the timer for 2 minutes on 'manual'. When finished allow the pressure valve to release on its own.

A small bottle wrapped and labelled beautifully makes a great and personal gift.

I'm jumping on the activated charcoal bandwagon, but not in the form of trendy charcoal-grey waffles or ice cream. Activated charcoal is pretty potent stuff and is used to trap and remove toxins and chemicals from the body. It is so good that it is even used in emergency rooms around the world to treat poisoning and drug overdoses.

I make this drink when someone in the house is poorly with a tummy bug (or, dare I say, a hangover). As much as activated charcoal is a huge trend at the moment, it can cause damage if overused. It is important to note that because activated charcoal removes toxins it can also remove essential minerals and vitamins, so the idea is to remove toxins, not strip the body of necessary nutrients. This drink should never be taken with a meal or with medication or supplements.

ACTIVATED CHARCOAL LATTE

DAIRY-FREE/GLUTEN-FREE/KETO/PALEO/VEGAN

SERVES 1

250ml nut milk, full-fat coconut milk or Pumpkin Seed Mylk (page 265)

2 capsules of high-grade activated charcoal (open the capsule and empty out the powder)

1 tsp vanilla extract

1 tsp coconut oil

maple syrup, to taste (optional)

1 Put all the ingredients in a saucepan and mix together, then warm through over a medium heat. Serve with a dollop of tender loving care!

On a summer trip to France a few years ago, I met a lady at the market in Eygalières who was selling dried hibiscus flowers. In the usual market-seller way, she shoved a shot glass of ice-cold hibiscus tea into my sweaty hands and demanded I taste it. I was hooked: it was truly the most delicious tart, yet fruity, cranberry-like drink I'd tasted. I bought three bags of dried flowers on the spot and went home to recreate the delicious drink. I learned that the best way to draw flavour out of the flowers is through a cold brew. The magic happens slowly, and patience is needed. (Hibiscus tea is often recommended as a way to lower blood pressure, therefore it should only be drunk in moderation.)

COLD-BREW HIBISCUS TEA

DAIRY-FREE/GLUTEN-FREE/KETO/PALEO/VEGAN

MAKES 1 LITRE

4 heaped tbsp dried hibiscus flower petals

1 litre filtered water

honey, or maple syrup or sweetener, to taste

1 Put all the ingredients in a jug and mix together. Cover and leave to stand in the fridge for a minimum of 24 hours. Serve with ice.

When my girls were little we would take them out for group dinners with friends. Their dinner would start with a chocolate milkshake, and by the time their food arrived they were full and didn't want to eat it. Oh, how naive I was in those days. Nowadays, I make everything we consume count: everything that my family eats and drinks must add nutritional value to our bodies. Even something as simple as a chocolate milk drink in the right form can give so much nourishment.

CHOCOLATE MYLKSHAKES

DAIRY-FREE/GLUTEN-FREE/KETO/PALEO/VEGAN

SERVES 4

750ml Pumpkin Seed Mylk (page 265) or nut milk of choice

3 tbsp raw cacao powder

4 tbsp sweetener, or to taste (optional)

½ tsp pink salt

1 tbsp vanilla extract

TRY SOMETHING DIFFERENT

Add a scoop or two of protein powder for a deliciously refreshing post-workout drink.

1 Using either a blender or a hand whisk, mix all the ingredients together well and serve ice cold.

This is one of my favourite drinks, as it is a great alternative to coffee if you are on a keto diet and needing to increase your fat intake. It is also a fantastically soothing aid for a sore throat, as somehow it tastes like a hug when you are feeling all achy and down in the dumps. My girls always ask for mugs of this if they feel a cold coming on.

SOOTHING LEMON AND GINGER TEA

DAIRY-FREE/GLUTEN-FREE/KETO/PALEO/VEGAN

MAKES 1 CUP

a thumb-sized piece of fresh ginger, unpeeled, sliced

3 lemon slices

1 heaped tsp coconut oil

1 tsp raw honey

1 Put all the ingredients in a mug or teapot and add 250ml boiling water. Leave to cool until lukewarm.

2 Drink as much and as often as possible to soothe a sore throat and stay hydrated.

I'm not exactly sure where the COVID-19 lockdown dalgona coffee craze stemmed from – some would say TikTok; others argue that it's been around for ages in Korea. Regardless of where it came from, it certainly kept many of us photographers entertained in creating the perfect image during our time indoors.

This coffee is absolutely delicious served cold on a hot day, or you can heat the milk and have it as a little touch of comfort on a cold winter's night.

DAIRY-FREE DALGONA COFFEE

DAIRY-FREE/GLUTEN-FREE/KETO/PALEO/VEGAN

SERVES 1

250ml almond milk

2 tbsp instant coffee

2 tbsp honey, or coconut sugar or sweetener of your choice

a handful of ice cubes, if making it cold

1 If making a hot drink, heat the milk in a saucepan over a medium-high heat until just boiling.

2 Meanwhile, using an electric whisk (you could do this by hand but it will be a workout for the guns), mix together the coffee, honey and 2 tbsp hot water until it forms a thick, fluffy, gooey foam emulsion.

3 Three-quarters fill a glass with the either hot milk, or cold milk and ice, leaving space for the coffee. Top with the coffee emulsion. Serve.

ACKNOWLEDGEMENTS

It goes without saying that I need to give the biggest mama-bear thanks to my guys, Derek, Gemma and Kyra. I'm sure at one point during writing this book I overheard you nickname me Donna 'Please Taste This' Crous. You guys propped me up with the strongest support during my toughest times, both with cancer and when I didn't believe I would get this book written. Derek, you always believe in me (even when I don't) – you are my rock!

Thanks to Jenny Remington-Hobbs for teaching the Croushold about healthy eating so many years back when we so desperately needed the help; and Beryl King for unknowingly mentoring me when I was newly married about how to entertain like a domestic goddess and make guests feel welcome around our table. Also to Megan Faure, Tracy Anderson, Lorna and Patrick O'Brian, Trish Mitchell, Belinda Steyn, and Suzanna De Jager and Sue Leach for inspiring me every time we were invited to eat the most incredible meals in your homes.

To my preppers – Trish Mitchell, Sascha Payne, Michelle Hutchinson, Mel Lewis, Gina Clayton, Karen Morkel Brink, Belinda Steyn and Tracy Anderson – for being my sounding boards while writing. Having your different and, more importantly, honest opinions about flavour combinations, choice of dishes and general book-related questions really helped me to make informed decisions.

Thanks too to Dr Karen S. Lee, who was my introduction to the world of cookery books. Allowing me to shoot three of your books opened up my world into publications and my career in food photography. I will always be eternally grateful to you for trusting me with your babies.

To my cutest little cousins, Jess and Anna Spencer, for being such willing and happy little models. Many of these images were shot on location at Kim's Pig Pen Farm, Secretts Farm in Milford and Sue Leach's apple orchard.

A huge thanks to my incredible crew at Little, Brown: my commissioning editor Tom Asker, who spotted the diamond in the rough with my proposal, and Duncan Proudfoot, for giving me the chance to show you what I can do. Both of you were so understanding when I was diagnosed and just showed me so much empathy and patience during my treatment months. To Andrew Barron for creating a masterpiece we can all be proud of with the beautiful creative design; you turned my vision into breathtaking reality. And finally, but by no means last, a huge thank you to my fairy editing mothers, Zoe Carroll and Jan Cutler, for waving their magic editing wands over my words.

Finally, to my late mum, Carol de Goveia, and my grandma, Julie Milsom, both incredibly strong, courageous and fiercely independent women who disliked cooking. I wish you were able to see this book. You are both the wind beneath my wings!

Index